Word Up!

Word Up!

A Lively Look at English

Rob Kyff

"The Word Guy"

Writers Club Press
San Jose New York Lincoln Shanghai

Word Up!

Writers Club Press
an imprint of iUniverse.com, Inc.

For information address:
iUniverse.com, Inc.
620 North 48th Street, Suite 201
Lincoln, NE 68504-3467
www.iuniverse.com

ISBN: 0-595-12478-X

Printed in the United States of America

Dedicated to Janice—
for her wisdom, kindness and love.

Contents

Acknowledgments

No writer is an island. In creating this book, I've been inspired, enlightened and supported by scores of friends, colleagues, readers and family members, and I am deeply grateful for their help.

Most of the material in this book originally appeared in my twice-weekly column on language for the *Hartford Courant*. My editors in the features department at the *Courant*—Kyrie O'Connor, Stephanie Summers and Joe Nunes—have generously given me the opportunity to share my thoughts on language with thousands of readers. They have not only afforded me complete editorial freedom, but also improved my columns with their patient and precise editing.

Tracy Clark, my editor at Tribune Media Services, has guided my column through the pathways of national syndication, untangling computer glitches and snagging last-minute errors. I also owe a debt of gratitude to Mark Mathes, former managing editor of Tribune Media Services, who in 1995 had the courage to take a risk on syndicating my fledgling column.

My colleagues at Kingswood-Oxford School have been extremely supportive of my writing, both personally and professionally. Heads of School Tyler Tingley and Lee Levison have generously allowed me to teach part-time so that I could pursue my writing career. To my Kingswood-Oxford colleagues in the Trout Brook Writers Group, I owe a special debt for their advice, support and wisdom: Jim Cahalan, Laura Hansen, Alex Kraus, Gary Pandolfi, Patricia Rosoff and Ann Serow.

The late Warren Baird, a fellow teacher and close friend, offered many helpful suggestions and ideas for columns, and was my court of last resort in adjudicating grammatical disputes.

My friends David Brooks, Richard Caley, Richard Chiarappa, Jerry Chichester, Joe Duffy, Larry Roberts, Richard Sheehan and Joe Strayhorn, and my sisters Pamela Kyff and Lisa Kyff have all offered unflagging support and wise counsel on my many writing projects over the years.

I also thank the many readers of my column, both known and anonymous, whose ideas, suggestions, insights and complaints have .enriched, enlightened and inspired me.

I'm extremely grateful to the ever-vigilant and ever-cheerful Chris Liebig and my #1 fan Ron Peterson for their vigorous and meticulous proofreading of this book.

Finally, I thank my wife, Janice, who has not only contributed her extensive skills as a professional librarian in researching and verifying the material in my column, but has also sustained me through disappointment and success with her abiding faith in my writing and in me.

Introduction

When my 10-month-old daughter Allison recently said her first word, I welcomed her to the wonders of the English language…

Allison, your native tongue is the world's most influential language, not just because your country is so economically and militarily dominant, but because English is so hospitable and versatile.

The most democratic of languages, English readily and cheerfully welcomes new words from other lands, from the *boondocks* of Tagalog to the *tundra* of Lapp to the *oasis* of Egyptian. It's an equal opportunity absorber.

As you begin to speak, you'll have over 350,000 common words to choose from, far more than any other language offers. You'll discover that English is a fertile, unpredictable garden, sprouting wondrous new words every day, words that allow you to express ideas, feelings and images precisely, concisely and creatively.

Ten years ago, for instance, children couldn't speak of *noodling* an idea, *browsing* the *net,* or *morphing* an image in *cyberspace.* You can.

While irregular verbs (*write/wrote, bite/bit*) and mysterious idioms ("I've got my eye on you") may bewilder you, you'll find the grammatical structure of English relatively simple.

Unencumbered by the inflections and gender markers that burden many other languages, you'll be free to use *book* as a noun, a verb or an adjective without even changing its spelling or pronunciation. You'll also be able to convey subtle distinctions of meaning that some other languages don't allow, as in, "I speak," "I do speak," and "I am speaking."

And the beauty! Someday you'll explore your language with eloquent companions. You'll rejoice with William Butler Yeats in the "bee-loud glade," shiver with Emily Dickinson's "zero at the bone," and discover with William Shakespeare how "the native hue of resolution is sicklied o'er with the pale cast of thought."

Allison, the word you chose to say first is a good old Anglo-Saxon interjection, so sharp and clear it might have been your greeting to the English language itself: Hi!

Chapter 1—

Weird Words: Contronyms and Other Delights

If you dust a table, you take dust off it. But if you dust crops, you put dust on them.

How can this be?

Dust is a strange kind of word known as a "contronym"—a word that can have two opposite meanings.

But contronyms aren't the only words and phrases that are contradictory. There are the mysterious "lost positives," such as *kempt* and *couth;* the notorious "unantonyms," such as *inflammable* and *unloosen;* and the legendary "oxymorons" such as *bittersweet* and *jumbo shrimp.*

Let's take a walk on the weird side...

Contronyms: Jekyll and Hyde words

Who said English is logical?

When an alarm goes off, it makes a sound, but when that alarm then goes off, it stops making a sound. If we say Joe is a good looker who takes a good photo, we may mean either that he looks good in a photo or that he's a good observer and good photographer.

Look here. We all know words can sometimes mean two different things, but can a word have two meanings that are exact opposites?

I say yes—and I don't mean no. Pick a side. In this battle, you can either "go for" me (support me) or "go for" me (attack me). You can fight "with me" (alongside me) or "with me" (against me), but my point is "moot" (not debatable), and not "moot" (debatable).

We have met the enemy and it is language.

The qualified genius Richard Lederer (Question: does *qualified* mean competent or limited? In this case, competent.) has coined a word for such self-contradictory words: *contronyms*—literally, opposite words.

When you *trim* a Christmas tree, you add things to it, but when you *trim* a hedge, you remove things from it. If you *bag* a job you either get it or quit it. If you *seed* a field you put seeds into it, but if you *seed* a watermelon, you remove seeds from it. A castle that's *impregnable* is invulnerable to penetration, but a woman who's *impregnable* is capable of being impregnated.

How does this happen? Well, you see the daddy has to be with the mommy…Oh, you mean, how do words take on opposite meanings?

I'm of two minds on this. Either the meanings of two opposite words *cleave* (join), or the meaning of one word *cleaves* (splits) into two opposite meanings.

Now let's get practical and examine some real-life instances in which contronyms almost cause disasters.

"Why it's so hard to rent an apartment" blares a magazine headline. But the meaning of this clause is rent in two. Does it mean why it's so hard for a landlord to rent out an apartment, or why it's so hard for a tenant to rent one? (And, come to think of it, when a tenant begs a landlord to "please release me," should the landlord rip up the lease or renew it?)

Similarly, this sentence from a book review offers no release from confusion: "Their patriotism was tempered by John Wayne flicks." Does this mean their patriotism was increased by Wayne's movies, or lessened by them? The two rival meanings of *temper*—strengthen and moderate—are left to Duke it out.

Meanwhile, back at the ranch, I recently found myself writing this comment on a student paper: "You write clearly, if not eloquently." Did I mean the student came close to eloquence in his writing or that he achieved no eloquence at all? My own sentence was neither clear nor eloquent.

Perhaps in revenge, another student recently wrote this sentence about World War I: "America decided to fight with Britain and France." Did this mean we were their ally or their enemy?

(Sometimes, by the way, you can put the ambiguity of contronyms to good use. Asked to review an aspiring author's manuscript, for instance, a renowned writer responded slyly, "I shall waste no time in reading it.")

I hate to sanction ambiguity, but *sanction* is another contronym. The noun *sanction,* which comes from the Latin word *sanctus* (holy), can mean either approval ("we gave sanction to his project") or disapproval ("we placed sanctions on his project").

Until the past few years, the verb form of *sanction* has miraculously escaped this ambiguity, meaning only "to approve," as in "I hate to sanction ambiguity." But, during the early 1990s, when there was so much talk of imposing "sanctions" on Iraq, people started using the verb *sanction* as a shorthand way of saying "impose sanctions," as in "we sanctioned Saddam" or "sighted sub, sanctioned same."

Sanctioning this madness (now what did I mean by that?), I officially welcome *sanction* as a full-fledged member of the Jekyll and Hyde Hall of Fame. Allow me to introduce some other inmates:

- **take down**—When members of the Senate urge that a colleague's remarks be *taken down,* they don't mean the comments should be recorded. They mean they should be repudiated. This definition is probably derived from a *take down* in wrestling, a move that forces a standing opponent to the mat. Are you taking this down?

- **peruse**—Officially, *peruse* means to read thoroughly, but it's often used to mean its opposite, to read casually or to browse.

- **put out**—Does someone who wants to *put out* an idea intend to present it or to squelch it?

- **weather**—A ship *weathers* (withstands) a storm, but a harsh winter will *weather* (wear away) wood.
- **wind up**—If I say this section on contranyms is *winding up*, do I mean it's just getting going, or that it's ending? Hmmm…

Idiom's delight

Some of the craziest phrases in English are idioms—expressions that, when taken literally, make no sense. Here a bookish, middle-age man named Logic discusses this problem with his congenial but disheveled nephew Idiom.

Idiom: Hi, Uncle Logic! I've really missed not seeing you.

Logic: If you've really missed *not* seeing me, that actually means that you'd rather not see me.

Idiom: Ah, Uncle Loj, you know I didn't mean it that way. Anyway, I'm sorry I'm late. I got caught in a huge traffic bottleneck.

Logic: If the bottleneck had been huge, there would have been plenty of room to drive through it.

Idiom: Well, the traffic was so bad, I almost had an accident. It was a near miss.

Logic: A near *miss* would be the same as hitting someone. What you mean is a near hit. By the way, I thought you were going to get a haircut.

Idiom: That idea sort of fell between the cracks.

Logic: You mean fell *through* the cracks. If something falls between the cracks, it hits the boards on the floor.

Idiom: Let's just say I was speaking tongue in cheek.

Logic: When your tongue is placed in your cheek, you can't speak at all. Try it.

Idiom: Narahamahrnunar…OK, OK. I was just trying to put my best foot forward.

Logic: *Best* can only refer to three or more items. Unless you have three feet, you can only put your *better* foot forward.

Idiom: It goes without saying that you're too picky about literal meanings.

Logic: If it goes without saying, why did you say it?

Idiom: Look, don't you think we should mend our fences?

Logic: If we mend our fences, we'll be putting up stronger barriers between us.

Idiom: When it comes to idioms, I think you should put up or shut up!

Logic: That should be "put up *and* shut up." What you want me to do is to put up with your illogical idioms and also shut up about them too.

Idiom: Gotcha! In this case, *put up* means fight, as in "put up your dukes." So "put up *or* shut up" is logical.

Logic *(obviously upset):* I could care less!

Lost positives: paradox found

If an awkward gesture is ungainly, why isn't a graceful gesture gainly? If messy hair is disheveled, why isn't neat hair sheveled? If a misbehaving child is incorrigible, why isn't a well-behaved child corrigible?

The same kind of questions might be asked about words such as *disaster* (Is a success an "aster"?); *inept* (Is a skilled person "ept"?); *nonplused* (Is a composed person "plused"?); *disgruntled* (Is a contented person "gruntled"?); and *indelible* (Is something erasable "delible"?).

Nonexistent words, such as *gainly,* that appear to be the positive forms of existing words (*ungainly*) are sometimes called "lost positives." This term is based on the assumption that these words once existed but then vanished, leaving only their antonyms behind.

It's true that our old friend English, being only human, does occasionally misplace a word here and there. ("Gee," the Mother Tongue might mutter, "I know I've seen that adjective around here somewhere; maybe I left it in East Anglia back in the 12th century.")

For instance, English lost *demit* and *expede* somewhere along the way, but managed to retain their antonyms *commit* and *impede*. And, while the lost positive *ruth,* meaning kindness, is hardly ever heard anymore, we say *ruthless* all them time.

But some lost positives aren't lost at all; they're just traveling incognito. The *ept* of *inept,* for instance, is really our old friend *apt* (quick to learn), and the *ert* of *inert* comes from our familiar buddy *art* (activity or skill).

Other lost positives are no longer lost. For instance, *kempt* (Middle English for *comb*) and *couth* (Old English for *known*) have recently made comebacks in English as back-formations of their surviving antonyms *unkempt* and *uncouth*. *Kempt* now means tidy, and *couth* now means refined.

So, in some ways, the term *lost positives* is a misnomer (as opposed to a *nomer?*)

Reverse engines: a guilty bystander skates on thick ice

The first car I ever owned was a 1957 Chevy Bel Aire, a two-toned, high-finned beauty with a straight-six engine, a radio that worked, and one, tiny flaw: it ran only in reverse.

Despite this problem, my car was great shakes, and something to sneeze at. As soon as I saw "Backy," as I quickly dubbed the car, I knew I would touch it with a ten-foot pole; it was my cup of tea. Though my friends' criticism of Backy was skin off my nose, I took it lying down. I still thought Backy was worth a hill of beans and a tinker's damn as well.

Driving Backy, I felt like a fish in water, as if I were in front of the eight ball, barking up the right tree. I was a spring chicken then, a young-timer for whom life was a laughing matter. At that time in my life, I had too few irons in the fire, was skating on thick ice, and was up to good. In fact, I was burning my candle at one end.

Don't get me wrong; I could be a little wild, too. One night I put on my worst bib and tucker, used low-falutin language, and headed out to trip the heavy fantastic in an unsafe haven. But when I threw Backy into gear, the car was rarin' to stop. Backy's low jinks seemed serious, and I decided solving this problem would be a brainer.

Luckily, at that moment, an old whippersnapper and a young codger happened by—two guys I knew from Adam. Dry behind their ears, they made bones about the fact that they were born yesterday. Though they looked as if they would hurt a fly, I gave these guilty bystanders long shrift. In return, they gave me the time of day and, as mechanics, proved they could cut the mustard.

Getting warm feet and biting off less than they could chew, these sung heroes fixed Backy. Soon all three of us were off on a domesticated goose chase, giving a narrow berth to profane cows along the way, and proving that we could hit the broad sides of barns, and see the forest for the trees.

As Backy zoomed along in reverse, I was awake at the switch, going with the grain, and learning that life was a holds-barred contest, an easy row to hoe and something to write home about.

Unantonyms: why inflammable *means flammable*

If fabric *ravels*, it frays, but if fabric *unravels*, it also frays. *Inflammable* substances ignite as easily as *flammable* ones, and *shameless* and *shameful* both mean disgraceful.

Wait a minute. Aren't the prefixes *in-* and *un-*, and the suffix *-less* supposed to give words an opposite meaning?

Not always.

You've heard of the Uncola? Welcome to the "unantonyms."

True enough, in most cases the prefixes *in-*, *im-*, *un-*, *dis-* and *non-*, and the suffix *-less* do turn words into antonyms. But sometimes these foxy "fixes" actually intensify rather than negate a word's meaning.

Inflammable, for instance, which appears to mean not able to catch fire, actually means able to catch fire. That's why it's safer to write *flammable* rather than *inflammable* on containers carrying ignitable substances. "But the sign said 'inflamma...'" BOOM!

Likewise, the *dis-* in *disgruntled* strengthens the meaning of its root word *grunt*, so that a disgruntled person grunts and grumbles a lot.

Other words with intensive prefixes include *inhabitable*, *unthaw*, *unstrip* and *unloosen*. While some experts argue that such prefixes are redundant and that only the root words (*habitable*, *thaw*, etc.) should be used, such unantonyms are well established in English.

But be careful. Some words with intensive prefixes or suffixes are not exact synonyms of their roots. *Invaluable*, for instance, means that something is more than valuable; it's so precious that its worth can't be measured. The same principle applies to *innumerable* and *numerous*.

Even *shameful* and *shameless* bear slightly different meanings. *Shameful* describes an act that causes disgrace. *Shameless* is an even stronger word, suggesting that the act seems to have been committed with absolutely no regard for its disgrace, as a shameless lie.

And while *passive* means receiving an action without responding, *impassive* means something slightly different—showing no emotion.

So don't become raveled trying to unravel the intricacies of unantonyms. Just jump, impassively, into the fray.

Oxymorons: the yoke's on you!

A dialogue between a sophomore and a student teacher…

Sophomore: Hey, teach! Did you watch the Arnold Schwarzenegger movie *True Lies* on cable last night? Awful good, huh?

Student Teacher: You bet. Did you know its title is an oxymoron?

Soph: An oxy…what?

Teach: Oxymoron—a word or phrase that joins two contradictory concepts. The word *oxymoron* itself is an oxymoron because it's formed from the Greek roots *oxus*, meaning sharp, and *moros*, meaning dull or foolish. We use oxymorons all the time. For instance, you just said *awful good.* And *sophomore* (wise fool) is an oxymoron, and so is *student teacher.*

Soph: So you and I are both oxymorons? Cool! But why would someone create an oxymoron anyway?

Teach: Poets and playwrights often use them to express the bittersweet ironies and ambiguities of life. William Shakespeare gave us *sweet sorrow,* John Milton *darkness visible,* Alfred, Lord Tennyson *falsely true,* William Butler Yeats *terrible beauty,* and Ernest Hemingway *scalding coolness.*

Oxymorons are used in politics, too—sometimes as nicknames, such as the *Little Giant* (Stephen Douglas) or *Iron Magnolia* (Rosalynn Carter), and sometimes to make one thing appear to be another: *peace offensive, build down* and *negative growth.*

Soph: *Good grief!* That *open secret* is the *living end.* Politicians must think Americans are *profoundly superficial.*

Teach: I'm *terribly pleased* to see you're catching on. There's a *tiny army* of oxymorons we use all the time, often without even realizing their inherent contradictions: *sight unseen, small fortune, jumbo shrimp* (and the double oxymoron *fresh frozen jumbo shrimp*), *taped live, old news, industrial* *park, working vacation, plastic silverware, random order, tight slacks, civil war, militant pacifist* and *lead balloon.*

Soph: So when my parents say that phrases like *nonworking mother, rock music, military intelligence, business ethics* and *educational television* are oxymorons, they're suggesting that these are contradictions in terms.

Teach: And how! Say, speaking of television, are you going to catch *Little Big Man* on cable tonight?

Soph: Nah. I'll be watching *Back to the Future.*

Some quizzical expressions

Pop quiz! Choose the correct word in these sentences illustrating common usage errors. (Answers and explanations follow, but no (peaking, peeking).

1) Surprise quizzes have always made me (nauseous, nauseated).
2) The (amount, number) of errors in these sentences is incredible.
3) In her speech, she (implied, inferred) that the law was weak.
4) She made several (illusions, allusions) to classical literature.
5) The jury found the testimony to be (credible, creditable).
6) Despite his dad's encouragement, the boy remained (disinterested, uninterested) in baseball.
7) I was able to (site, cite) several examples to support my argument.
8) The philanthropist gained (notoriety, fame) for his generosity.

Answers:

1) Nauseated. Using *nauseous* to mean sick nauseates most purists. *Nauseous* means disgusting, as in a "nauseous odor."
2) Number. *Amount* refers to singular words ("amount of grain"), while *number* is used for plural items ("number of errors").
3) Implied. *Imply* means to suggest something; *infer* means to interpret something from someone else's statement.

4) Allusions. An allusion is a reference to something else; an illusion is mistaken idea or perception.

5) Credible. *Credible* means believable; *creditable* means worthy of credit, admirable.

6) Uninterested. *Disinterested* means impartial; *uninterested* means lacking interest. A good trial judge should be disinterested, but not uninterested.

7) Cite. *Cite* means to refer to something; the noun *site* is a location, while the verb *to site* means to place something on a site.

8) Fame. *Notoriety* bears a distinctly negative connotation. Bandits gain notoriety; philanthropists gain fame.

Scores: 8—you peaked! (or peeked); 6–7—you earn a citation; 4–5—you're creditable; 0–4—you're seeking notoriety.

Chapter 2—

Predicate Predicaments:
A Guide to Troublesome Verbs

Quick!

Should you say:

"I'm lying down" or "I'm laying down"?

"This will effect me" or "This will affect me"?

"I'm flouting the rules" or "I'm flaunting the rules"?

If you're like most people, you probably had a hard time coming up with the correct verb. Nothing in English is more vexing than these easily confused verbs. It makes you wonder whether someone along the line didn't deliberately concoct these look-alikes just to insure, er…ensure that we'd be driven crazy.

Let's examine some villainous verbs.

Affect/effect

No pair of words causes more usage problems than *affect* and *effect*. This devilish duo bumbles through the linguistic landscape like Laurel and Hardy, getting into "another fine mess" wherever they go.

Using these words incorrectly will hardly earn you usage laurels.

Time to effect a solution, you say? I'll try to have some effect.

Affect and *effect* cause trouble for several reasons: Both can be used as verbs and nouns; both are related in meaning; both sound alike…you get the idea.

The verb *affect* means to influence or to make an impression on something, as in, "This law will affect the life of almost every citizen."

The verb *effect* means to bring about or produce. Thus, "The law-makers tried to effect a solution to the problem," or "The chemist tried to effect a solution."

Be careful, because misuse of these verbs can cause meanings opposite to those intended. When you seek to affect problems, for instance, you try to eliminate them. But if you seek to effect problems, you try to cause them.

As for nouns, *effect* is almost always the word you should use. It means product or result, whether you're talking about the result of an attempt to effect something or affect something. So whether you *affect* or *effect,* you're doing it only for *effect.*

The noun *affect* is sometimes used by psychologists to mean emotion or feeling. They like to couch their descriptions in jargony sentences such as "The patient showed no affect when she discussed her compulsive misuse of *affect* and *effect.*"

Another confusing twist is the use of the verb *affect* to mean put on airs or pretend. Thus, "Peter affects a British accent," means he pretends to have one, not that he influences one.

Given all these complications, it's no wonder some of us have to affect an understanding of *affect* and *effect.*

Bring/take

In the world of usage, there's always plenty of give and take over the use of *bring* and *take.*

Be sure to use *bring* whenever something is being conveyed *to* the person speaking. Saying, "Please bring your football home," for instance, means the speaker wants the football brought to her.

Be sure to use *take* whenever something is being conveyed *away from* the person speaking. Saying, "Please take your football home," means the speaker wants the football taken away from her. Thus, a parent who tells a child to "take the stray puppy home" means something very different than the parent who tells the child to "bring the stray puppy home."

Problems with *bring* and *take* often arise when the speaker's position is ambiguous or irrelevant. For instance, let's say a husband and wife are leaving for a cocktail party, and the husband tells his wife to "bring your beeper with you." His use of *bring* instead of *take* is not necessarily wrong; it merely suggests that he is thinking of the future, when they're already at the party and his wife might need her beeper. In this case, the direction implied by *bring* or *take* is essentially irrelevant and the meaning is still clear.

Can/may

Billy: Mrs. Sumpweed, can I go the bathroom?

Mrs. Sumpweed: Of course you *can* go the bathroom, Billy. You're able to walk, the classroom door works, the hallway is unobstructed, the boys' bathroom door is unlocked and the plumbing works. The question you meant to ask is, "May I go to the bathroom?"

Billy: "May *you* go to the bathroom?" Why, Mrs. Sumpweed, I think it would be highly inappropriate for me, a mere student, to presume to ask a question like that on your behalf. I mean, I'd feel very awkward...

Mrs. Sumpweed: Can it! I mean, *may* it. I mean, you should use *may* when you're referring to permission to do something, and *can* when you're referring to the possibility of doing something. Thus, while you certainly can go to the bathroom, whether you may or not depends upon my say so.

Billy: You don't say.

Susie: Excuse me, Mrs. Sumpweed, but my big brother told me that the distinction between *can* and *may* is one of those outmoded schoolroom edicts that nobody pays any attention to in everyday speech. He says we can say, "Can I have a cookie?" and everyone will know that we mean, "May I have a cookie?"

Mrs. Sumpweed: I don't like to be a *may*-sayer, but the question is not whether you *can* say, "Can I have cookie," it's whether you *may* say it. In certain contexts, such as corporate reports, newspaper editorials and grammar books, you definitely may not.

Billy: Uh, Mrs. Sumpweed...

Susie: But even grammarians sometimes use *can* to indicate permission. For instance, a language expert once wrote, "*Substitute* can only be followed by *for*" when, technically, he should have written, "may only be followed." And, besides, isn't it kind of snooty to insist on *may* all the time? Which sounds more generous and friendly, "You can use my crayons anytime" or "You may use my crayons anytime"?

Billy: Mrs. Sumpweed, I really need...

Mrs. Sumpweed: I still say it's a distinction worth preserving. *Can* can only be used to indicate possibility, not permission...er...I mean, *can* may only be used to indicate possibility, not permission.

Billy: May Day! May Day!

Mrs. Sumpweed: You may

Comprise/compose

Comprise, which is often misused to mean to make up or to constitute, actually means to include or embrace.

Speaking of making up and embracing, you must remember this, a kiss is just a kiss. And you must remember this as well: The whole comprises the parts; the parts compose the whole. I'll play it again, Sam: The whole comprises the parts; the parts compose the whole.

For instance, this answer to your question *comprises* sentences; sentences *compose* this answer. (Actually, I composed this answer, but I'll let the sentences take credit this time.)

To put it another way, here's what your parents never told you about the birds and the bees: Birds compose a flock, and a flock comprises birds. Bee hives compose an apiary, and an apiary comprises hives.

But just because you've mastered the proper use of *comprise*, and would never write a sentence such as "bacon, lettuce and tomato comprise a BLT," you still think you can get away with using comprise in the passive voice by writing "a BLT is *comprised of* bacon, lettuce and tomato."

You old devil, you! You're like a patient who, told by a doctor to lay off bacon, cheats by sneaking a BLT. By trying to hide your forbidden *comprise* between the tomato of a suffix (*-ed*) and the lettuce of a preposition (*of*), you think you've concealed your crime from me.

But The Word Guy sees all! Here are a couple of recent examples that really bring home the bacon: "Over half of our transcontinental fleet is now comprised of spacious Boeing 757s and 767s"; "The group's board is comprised of the nation's regional school accreditation agencies, as well as the national association of elementary, middle school and secondary principals."

Let us return to primary principles:

1) *Comprise* means to include, contain, or embrace components. A BLT comprises bacon, lettuce and tomato. The Beatles comprised John, Paul, George and Ringo.

2) *Compose* means to make up, constitute, form. Bacon, lettuce and tomato compose a BLT. John, Paul, George and Ringo composed most of their own songs.

3) Because *comprise* means to contain, you can't get away with using it in the passive voice ("comprised of"). You wouldn't say, "a BLT is "included of," "contained of," or "embraced of" bacon, lettuce and tomato, so it doesn't make sense to say it's "comprised of" these

items either. Say, "it's composed of bacon, lettuce and tomato" instead. (Say it's composed of beets, kelp and broccoli. Would you still eat it?)

Aaaah, you say, these are just silly rules teachers and doctors make up to worry you. "Don't eat bacon!" "Don't use *comprised of* when you mean composed of!" I can't heed them all. Which one should I follow?

My BLT (bottom-line thought): I'd rather have a usage infraction than a coronary infarction.

Ensure/insure

"Rotating your tires will insure normal wear."

Is *insure* used correctly in this sentence? Or should it be *ensure?* Some of us are unsure.

Traditionally, *insure* has been reserved only for references to financial matters. You insure your house, your life and your jewelry.

Ensure is supposed to have a more general meaning: to make sure of. Thus, you take precautions to ensure safety, or you proofread to ensure accurracy, er...accuracy.

But lately, more and more people are using *insure* as a synonym for *ensure,* giving us sentences about *insuring* the normal wear of tire tread.

Speaking of tread, permissivists rush in where angels fear to, so I'll don the halo of conservatism on this one. My reason: observing the distinction between *ensure* and *insure* prevents ambiguous sentences such as, "We want to insure your success." Does this "insurer" want to make sure we succeed, or to write up a policy protecting the assets our success has produced?

That's why most careful writers make it a policy to ensure proper meaning by using *ensure,* not *insure,* when they mean to make sure of.

Here are two other confusing *e/i* verbs:

- **evoke/invoke**—*Evoke* means to draw forth or to call to mind, as in "His speech evoked pride in the audience," or "The novel evokes the antebellum South." *Invoke* means to call on something for assistance or to apply a law, as in "The priest invoked the gods," or "The mayor invoked an obscure ordinance."

- **emigrate/immigrate**—*Emigrate* refers to a migration *from* someplace: "They emigrated from France." *Immigrate* refers to a migration *to* someplace: "They immigrated to the U.S." But remember, "Jill emigrated to the U.S." is correct if you're speaking from the perspective of the country Jill is leaving; likewise, "Jill immigrated from France" is correct if you're speaking from the perspective of the country Jill is entering.

Flaunt/flout

I never thought I'd cite a TV commercial as an example of proper word usage, but here goes. The old Braniff Airlines ads had it right: "If you've got it, flaunt it." (Unfortunately, Braniff proved better at sloganeering than solvency.)

Flaunt, a word of unknown origin, means to show off ostentatiously. *Flout*, from the Old English *flouten*, means to display contempt or scorn, usually for a law or social convention. You can flaunt your mastery of usage by not flouting this distinction.

Recently I've been flabbergasted at the number of usage errors involving words beginning with the letters *fl.* I'll flagellate the most flagrant flubs:

- **flounder/founder**—These two verbs have been confused and misused ever since the days of the founding fathers (or "floundering fathers," depending on your view of American history.)

To *flounder* is to thrash around in a clumsy or confused way, like a fish out of water or the U.S. government under the Articles of

Confederation. To *founder*, which comes from the Latin word *fundus* (bottom), is to sink or collapse. Thus, if a pitcher flounders, warm up the bullpen; if a pitcher founders, warm up the showers.

- **flay/flail**—Because these words are so similar in meaning, it's hard to flay or flail anyone for failing to distinguish between them.

  Flay means to strip off the skin or outer covering, often by whipping or lashing; metaphorically, it means to criticize severely. When your boss has flayed you, you feel as if she has filleted you.

  Flail, which originally referred to a device for threshing grain, means to strike or beat violently, or to wave or swing vigorously. When cars break down, many drivers flail their steering wheels and then flail their arms at passing cars for help. But whatever you do, never flay your arms at passing cars. It's too melodramatic—and very painful.

Gibe/jibe/jive

Gibe means to taunt, heckle or jeer someone. On the ridicule scale, it's somewhere between *deride* and *kid*, as in "The students gibed the teacher for his ignorance of usage distinctions, but, being totally secure and confident, he was impervious to their gibes."

Jibe is a nautical term that means to shift a sail from one side to the other in order to change direction (tack). It also means to be in agreement or accord, as in "your definition jibes with mine." This second meaning may be anchored in the nautical definition, perhaps because the tacks of a sailboat blend or jibe to produce its overall course.

But, to jibe just a bit, *jibe* has long been an accepted alternative spelling for *gibe*. In fact, the use of *jibe* to mean ridicule dates back to Shakespeare's time. When Hamlet, engaging in a bit of philosophical skullduggery, asks Yorick gravely, "Where be your jibes now?" he's not referring to the dead jester's nautical tactics or his skill with a single scull. He's asking, tongue in cheekbone, "Where are your taunts now?"

Jive, which originally meant jazz music or the slang used by jazz musicians, has been extended to any deceptive, nonsensical or glib talk. Hey, like, man, you dig? Thus, we say, "They were just talking jive," or "Don't try to jive me." More recently, *jive* has been used as an adjective to mean phony, as in "He's a jive dude."

Because *jive* carries this connotation of misleading smooth talk, it's easy to see why it's often confused with *jibe*. After all, if you jive people enough, they might be convinced that your ideas jibe with theirs.

Lay/lie

Everyone misuses *lie* and *lay* occasionally, and anyone who tells you otherwise is either lying or laying an ego trip on you.

I wish we could let all sleeping dogmas lie, but some purebred grammarians bark doggedly when we confuse these verbs. Most of us, of course, have no trouble mastering the distinction between the intransitive verb *lie*, meaning to recline ("I lie on the couch"), and the transitive verb *lay*, meaning to place or put down ("I lay the book on the table.")

The problem lies in the fact that the past tense of the irregular verb *lie* is *lay*, as in, "Yesterday, I lay on the couch." Usually, when we reach for the past tense of a verb in English, even an irregular verb, we want one of those hairy-chested verbs ending in a hard *d*: *die-died, try-tried*. That's why we want the past tense of *lie* to be *lied* or *laid*, and not the wimpy sounding *lay*.

To make us even more tense, the past participle tense of *lie* is the funny sounding *lain* ("I have lain on the couch"), while both the past and past participle tenses of *lay* are *laid*.

When it comes to this usage issue, lay people like songwriters and authors have mostly lain down on the job. Bob Dylan and Joan Didion, for instance, laid grammatical eggs when they wrote the song "Lay, Lady, Lay" (should be "Lie, Lady, Lie") and the novel *Play It as It Lays* (should be "as It Lies"), respectively. In fact, Didion's title reinforces the popular misconception that people who are reclining *lie* and objects that are reclining *lay*, and since we're playing winter golf rules, her bad lie could stand some improvement.

But, if you think you'll never have a prayer of developing a foolproof *lay-lie* detector, here's one: "Now I lay me down to sleep." If the direct object *me* weren't there, it would be "Now I lie down to sleep," but since the *me* is there, and you are, in essence, laying your body down to sleep, *lay* is correct.

No lie.

Loan/lend

For three centuries, language experts have denounced the use of *loan* as a verb to mean lend, as in, "I'll loan you some money."

During the 18th century, for instance, British linguists instructed their American colonists, "Neither a borrower nor a loaner be." But Americans, being a nation of defiant "loners," showed little interest in this usage dictate—and paid even less interest on the money the Brits had "loaned" them.

Even distinguished American writers freely used *loan* to mean lend: Robert Frost ("loan you his copy"), William Faulkner ("had loaned money to the town"), and Andy Rooney ("loan him the eighty dollars"). In fact, the use of *loan* as a verb is no longer considered incorrect.

Rear/raise

"Goats are raised and children are reared," say the usage purists. But, as anyone who has brought up small children knows, there's often little difference between kids and kids.

Once again, it's the British who first raised the *rear* issue, condemning "raise children" as a provincial Americanism. But, Americans, whether they believe in spanking or not, have always preferred to raise their children rather than rear them. So today, those insisting on *rear* find themselves fighting a rear-guard action.

Stanch/staunch

The verb stanch is often confused with the adjective staunch. Because both stanch and staunch evolved from the Latin root *stans, stare,* meaning to stand, the meaning of both words involves the concept of standing firmly—either for or against something.

The verb *stanch* means to stop or check the flow of something, often a liquid like blood or tears, as in "The medic stanched the flow of blood from the soldier's ear." But sometimes an emotion or trend is said to be stanched, as in "Joining Toastmasters stanched her fear of public speaking."

The adjective *staunch* means dedicated and steadfast, usually in devotion to a person, cause or duty, as in, "John Brown was a staunch abolitionist," or (as an adverb), "Mary Elizabeth Lease staunchly defended the Populist cause." Of all the words designating loyalty or faithfulness, *staunch* is the staunchest.

In fact, *stanch and staunch* were once used interchangeably. Technically, it's still OK to switch them, but anyone who speaks of "staunching the flow of blood" or of a "stanch supporter" is taking a stance that will stun staunch standard bearers.

Reaching an agreement

If you'll agree to be a subject, I'll subject you to this trial-and-error quiz on the subject of subject-verb agreement.

1) The jury foreman, John Subject, as well as nine other jurors, (is, are) certain the defendant is guilty.

2) However, Mary Verb—and her fellow juror Pete Predicate—(is, are) unsure about the defendant's guilt.

3) None of the other ten jurors (is, are) in agreement with Mary and Pete.

4) Neither Mary nor Pete (is, are) certain that the key witnesses are telling the truth.

5) Neither of these two jurors (is, are) willing to vote for conviction.

6) They believe that either the defendant or the witnesses (is, are) lying.

7) This is one of those situations that (is, are) unlikely to produce agreement between Subject and Verb.

Answers:

1) Is. Don't fall for the old "as well as" trick. A singular subject followed by *as well as, together with, with, in addition to* or *accompanied by* still takes a singular verb.

2) Is. Dash the notion that additional items—set off by dashes—make the subject plural. They don't.

3) Are. The *none* issue has become a non-issue. You may have been raised to believe that *none*, being a contraction of *no one* or *not one*, should always take a singular verb. Now none of the experts are insisting on this.

4) Is. Don't ig"nor" this: singular subjects joined by *or* or *nor* take a singular verb.

5) Is. When *neither* or *either* appears by itself and is not part of an *or* or *nor* phrase, it's not an either-or situation. Always use a singular verb.

6) Are. Location, location, location! When a singular and a plural subject are joined by *or* or *nor*, the verb agrees with the subject that's nearer to it.

7) Are. Even though you might think the *one* in the phrase *one of those* would demand a singular verb, *one of those* always takes a plural verb. Reverse the sentence and you'll see why: "Of those situations that are unlikely to produce agreement between Subject and Verb, this is one."

Chapter 3—

Ety'myth'ology: Exposing Erroneous Word Origins

If you believe *cop* is an acronym for "constable on patrol" or that *posh* stands for "port out, starboard home," or that *sirloin* got its name from being knighted "Sir Loin," you've studied ety"myth"ology, not etymology.

Let's have a *lark* (no, it's not from the bird) as we light *bonfires* (from "bone fire," not the French "bon") under some common myths about word derivations. We'll prove that many folk etymologies are pure *hogwash* (which refers not to bath water for pigs but to their swill—liquid leftovers and solid scraps). (I"m indebted to Hugh Rawson's wonderful book *Devious Derivations* for much of the material in this chapter.)

- **andiron**—The French word for a stand that holds logs in a fireplace is *andier*, and the English (who apparently liked pumping iron into any word they could) mistook the *ier* in *andier* for *iron*. Because an *andier* was likely to be made of iron, it too was ruthlessly stuffed into English's *iron* maiden.

- **Beefeaters**—In searching out esoteric etymologies, linguists often ignore the obvious. The name *Beefeaters* for the London guards, for instance, has been painstakingly traced to the French *buffetier*, keeper of the cupboard. In fact, it's simpler: the guys ate beef.

- **buckaroo**—Sorry, pardner. This word for a cowboy has nothing to with the bucking of a cowboy from his horse or with buckskin. *Buckaroo* is an American rendition of *vaquero*, the Spanish word for cowboy.

- **buttery**—Because a buttery is a large room for storing food at a school or college, you might be tempted to assume it's derived from *butter*. Butter not. *Buttery* is a rebottling of the Middle English word *botterie* (bottle) and originally referred to a room where liquors were stored in bottles or casks. Another genie let out of the *bottle*, by the way, is *butler* (*boutellier* in French), someone who, among other duties, delivers bottles.

- **cabal**—Many people base their etymology for *cabal* on an initial assumption: It was an acronym derived from the last names of King Charles II's five most influential ministers (Clifford, Arlington, Buckingham, Ashley and Lauderdale.) Actually, these are the first names of Scarlett O'Hara's husbands.

  But the plot thickens. Linguists discovered that *cabal* comes from the Hebrew word *cabala*, a Jewish religious philosophy based on an esoteric interpretation of Hebrew scriptures. In the English word *cabal*, this notion of an esoteric or secret intrigue still survives, which is a lot more than you can say for most members of cabals.

- **cat's cradle**—This children's game of stretching strings in various patterns between the hands was probably first called *cratch* or *cratch-cradle*, *cratch* being an old word for a rack or manger. Though a brave cat might indeed be able to lounge in such a small cradle, a thorough CAT scan of this term's origins has revealed no connection to *cat*.

- **cop**—No acronym for *Constable on Patrol*, it's copped from the verb *cop*, meaning to catch.

- **coward**—Though the idea that *coward* is derived from the easily frightened animal called a *cow* is "udderly" ridiculous, *coward* did come from animal behavior. It high-tailed into English from the old French *coe* (tail) because a scared animal shows its tail as it flees.

- **crayfish**—The freshwater crustacean called the *crayfish* is clearly not a fish, so there must be something fishy about the origins of this word. There is. In the 14th century, when Middle English speakers adopted the Old French word for this creature (*crevise*, pronounced "cray-veece"), they e"fish"iently turned its second syllable into a familiar word: fish. (Hey, they reasoned, the thing lives in the water, right?) And so *crevise* sunk to *crayfish*.

- **cutlet**—*Cutlet* has nothing to do with a butcher knife. It comes from the French *cotellete*, which, in turn, comes from the Latin root *costa*, meaning the side of something, as in a seacoast or a lamb's rib. So *cutlet*, if you can stand a little ribbing, is actually a little rib, not a little cut.

- **down in the dumps**—You'll be glad to know that the dumps you sometimes feel down in have nothing to do with garbage.

  The melancholy *dumps* comes from the Dutch *domp*, meaning haze or mist, because a sad person seems to be in a gloomy fog. The garbage *dump* comes from the Middle English *dompen*, meaning to drop or fall. So, no matter how down in the dumps you feel, refuse to feel like refuse.

- **ears of corn**—Many people assume ears of corn are so named because they protrude from stalks the way human ears protrude from heads. But there's not a kernel of evidence to support this corny th"ear"y. In fact, the anatomical *ear* and the corn *ear* sprout from completely different roots.

  The bodily *ear* comes from the Latin *auris*, which also gives us *aural* and *auricle*. The corny *ear* comes from the Indo-European root *ak*, meaning sharp. *Ak*, the root that gives us words like *acute* and *acrid*, became *ahuz* in early Germanic languages, and *ahuz* evolved into *aehher* and eventually *ear* in English. So ears of corn are so named, not because they resemble human ears, but because they protrude sharply from their stalks.

- **egg on**—This phrase has nothing to do with eggs. It comes instead from the Old Norse *eggja*, meaning to edge, and is a contraction of *edge on*, which once meant to incite or provoke.

- **eleventh hour**—Most people assume this phrase for a last-minute effort, such as "an eleventh-hour agreement," refers to the hour between 11 p.m. and midnight, even though that's technically the 12th hour (after noon).

  In fact, *eleventh hour* refers, not to the eleventh hour after midnight or noon, but from the eleventh hour of a work shift. The term comes from Jesus' parable (Matthew 10:1-16) about the boss who paid the same wage to workers who arrived at the eleventh hour of the work day (between 4 p.m. and 5 p.m.), as he did to those who had already put in ten hours.

- **getting down to brass tacks**—Some say this expression refers to the tacks used in upholstery. But the earl of etymology, Charles Earle Funk, says those who advance such tacky theories are being naughty when they should be nautical.

  According to his Funky explanation, the brass tacks referred to are most likely the copper bolts on the hull of a ship, which are exposed when the hull is completely scraped of barnacles. Thus, someone who clears away all debris and gets to the bottom of something is getting down to brass tacks.

- **good scout**—Being a good scout, I'm always eager to assist an elderly but accurate etymology across the street. The term *good scout*, which predates the Sir Robert Baden-Powell's founding of the Boy Scouts in 1908, probably derives from the use of *scout* to mean servant. So Sir Robert's butler was probably a good scout before his (scout) master was.

- **greyhound**—A greyhound is named, not for its color, but for its speed. *Greyhound* is derived from the Old Norse *greyhundr*. In *greyhundr*, *hundr* meant hound, but *grey* meant, not the color grey, but a coward. The reasoning seems to be that greyhounds run fast because they're afraid. So you might say a greyhound runs fast because it's yellow.

- **gridiron**—*Gridiron* comes from the Middle English *gridirne*, meaning a griddle (a pan or flat metal surface used for cooking by dry heat). The *irne* part of *gridirne* had nothing to do with iron, but, because a gridirne was sometimes made of iron, people assumed the word was a combination of *grid* and *iron*. Through the miracle of the Bessemer process, this eventually led to *gridiron* and the Pittsburgh Steelers.

- **hangnail**—This word comes from the Anglo-Saxon word *angnaegl*, which originally meant a corn on your foot that's so painful you feel as if you've stepped on an iron nail. Eventually, *angnaegl* also came to describe the irritating flap of skin near the base of a fingernail or toenail.

  Then, in a double whammy of linguistic obliteration, the *ang* (corn) was misunderstood as *hang*, and the *naegl* (iron nail) was transformed into a human nail, to give us *hangnail*. So, for want of a *naegl*, the iron nail was lost, and for want of an *ang*, the corn was lost…you get the hang of it.

- **hooker**—Though often said to be derived from the prostitutes who followed the army of Gen. Joseph Hooker during the Civil War, this term was walking the streets well before the war started.

- **husky**—The theory that the dogs that pull Arctic sleds are called *huskies* because they're so big and sturdy is sheer mush. *Husky* is actually a mispronunciation of *Eskimo*, a people who prefer to be called *Innuit*.

- **in a pickle**—This expression is derived, not from the shriveled cucumber we call a pickle, but from the brine and vinegar in which it sits. Because this liquid is also called a *pickle*, anyone stuck in a tight spot is said to be in a pickle.

This usage in English may have been influenced by the Netherlands phrase *in de pekel zitten* (sit in the pickle). So someone in a pickle may also be in Dutch.

- **malinger**—Someone who malingers (fakes illness) may linger around the house (at least until the school bus leaves). But *linger* lingers not in *malinger*, which actually comes from the French *malingre* (sickly).

- **nickname**—Almost every Tom, Nick and Harry assumes that a nickname is so called because it's nicked from a longer name. Nix that. *Nickname* is a mispronunciation of the 13th-century word *eke-name*, meaning also name or another name.

- **nightmares**—They have nothing to do with horses. *Mare* was an Old English word for demon, while our word *mare* comes from *mearh*, the Old English word for horse.

- **OK**—Language historians have been debating the origins of this distinctly American term since it first appeared during the mid-19th century. Over the years, *OK* has been attributed variously to the initials of Old Keokuk (an Indian chief), Obadiah Kelly (a shipping agent) or Orrins-Kendall (a favorite brand of 19th-century cracker). Others have suggested *OK* evolved from the Finnish word *oikea*, the Haitian *Aux Cayes* (a premium rum) or the Chocta Indian *okey* (meaning, "it is so").

The most convincing explanation came from Columbia University professor Allen Walker Read in 1941. Tracking *OK*'s first use in print to a Boston newspaper of 1839, Read determined that *OK* evolved from young Bostonians' trendy habit of abbreviating deliberately misspelled phrases such as *oll wright* (*O.W.*) and *oll korrect* (*O.K.*)

OK came into common use a year later when President Martin Van Buren, nicknamed "Old Kinderhook" for his home town in New York State, ran for a second term. His supporters joined OK Clubs, and "OK" became their national rallying cry. Though he was *OK*, Van Buren lost.

• **p's and q's**—Every field of intellectual endeavor seems to have at least one, ongoing, unresolved controversy. In astronomy, it's the origin of the universe. In philosophy, it's the nature of consciousness.

In etymology, it's the origin of the expression "Mind your *p*'s and *q*'s." Charles Funk, a linguist who minds his *p*'s and *q*'s more carefully than most, discovered no fewer than five different creation scenarios:

Scenario #1—Stern-faced pedagogue to first-graders: "Now children, don't confuse letters that look alike. Mind your *p*'s and *q*'s."

First grader's note to classmate: "Do you think there'll be a qoq puiz?"

Scenario #2—Stern-faced printer to apprentices: When you ink-stained wretches are setting type, don't mistake a *p* for a *q*. We live in the Goode Olde Days when type is still set in reverse, so this could easily happen.

Apprentice to co-worker: To hell with *p*'s and *q*'s, let's modernize the language by dropping the *e*'s from the ends of adjectives.

Scenario #3—Stern-faced bartender to patron in English pub: You've given me only 70 pence, Old Chap. On my account board, I've chalked you up for two *p*'s and three *q*'s, indicating you drank two pints and three quarts. That would be 80 pence.

Patron: My gooooood, man—hiccup—I aschtuaally drank shhree pintsssh and two quartsssh. Pleassshh mind *your*—'iccup—*p*'s and *q*'s.

Scenario #4—Stern-faced French dancing master to young gentlemen: "Watch your pieds (feet), s'il vous plait, and your queues (pigtails) as well, especially when bowing to Mademoiselle. Mind your *p*'s and *q*'s!

Student to partner: I'd like to invite you for dinner Saturday night to discuss whether a French abbreviation can ever be used in English. Can you RSVP by Friday?

Scenario #5—Stern-faced 16th-century wife to husband about to leave house in his pee coat (from Dutch *pij*, a coarse cloth, which gives us the name *pea jacket*): If the back of your pee coat gets soiled by the grease of your queue (pigtail), you'll be in Dutch. Mind your pee and queue. Husband: That explanation strikes me as an old husbands' tail.

Stern-faced author to reader: I've minded my *p*'s and *q*'s, but the origin of this phrase remains elusive.

• **pan (a play or book)**—Some authorities trace this phrase to 19th-century American prospectors who used metal pans to separate gold from sand and gravel. When no gold was found, miners would say their ore hadn't panned out. (Actually, when no gold was found these miners would say a lot of other words, most of them not suitable for minors.)

Anyway, soon theatrical and literary critics began writing that failed books and plays hadn't panned out, and, eventually, a critic who gave an artistic work a negative review was said to pan it.

But others say this expression may be no "miner" matter; in fact, it could be an either "ore" situation. Another possible explanation involves the top or pan of a tamping bar, which is repeatedly pounded or panned by a sledgehammer. So critics who hammered plays and books were said to be panning them.

Jumping into the frying pan, others say *pan* comes from cooking food in a kitchen pan. Thus, critics pan a play, book or film, the same way they fry bacon. Which may explain why an actor who has been panned as a ham feels like a piece of fried ham.

- **patter**—You might think that the patter at boring cocktail parties comes from the pitter-patter of little feats, but it's really a shortening of *Pater Noster*, Latin for "Our Father" in the Lord's Prayer.

- **pester**—Though *pester* has come to mean act like a pest, it originally had nothing to do with pest. Derived from the French word *empstrer* (hobbled), it once meant obstructed, clogged. But inevitably the meaning of *pester* came under the influence of *pest*. *Pester* lost its clogged denotation and came to mean annoy or harass.

- **piggyback**—*Piggyback* is a corruption of the 16th-century terms *pick back* and *pick pack*, which referred either to (take your pick): 1) a back that was picked to have a pack thrown on it; 2) a pack that was picked to be thrown on a back. Given this linguistic cat's cradle, it's no wonder people found it easier to say *piggyback*.

- **posh**—Wealthy English travelers booking sea passage to India, the story goes, would always try to reserve staterooms on the shady, and therefore, more comfortable side of the ship. Thus they requested "port out, starboard home," meaning they wanted the port side on the outward journey and the starboard side on the homebound voyage. The story goes that tickets for these more expensive rooms were thus stamped with the acronym *P.O.S.H.*, so *posh* became a synonym for elegant and fashionable.

  Unfortunately, experts sink this derivation of *posh*. They offer explanations that are much more boring: *posh* was British slang for money or it once meant dandy. But, when *posh* comes to shove, some say, don't give up the ship!

- **primrose**—A *primrose* is neither prim nor a rose. Because this flower was thought to be one of the first to bloom in spring, it was called *prima rosa* (first flower) in Latin. (Compounding this misnomer is the fact that a primrose isn't even one of the first flowers to bloom in spring. Oh well.)

- **quarry**—Stonecutters do seek out rocks with the vigor of hunters pursuing their quarry, but that's not why their excavation is called a *quarry*. A hunter's *quarry* comes from the French *cuiree*, the part of a slain animal's entrails fed to the hounds. A rock *quarry* is cut from the Old French *quarre* (squared stone).

- **racy**—The characters in racy novels may rush around with a fast crowd, but that's not why their sexy escapades are called *racy*. This *racy* is not to the swift *race* (from the Old Norse *ras*), but to the *race* that means type or kind (as in "human race"). The piquant tastes of certain races of fruits were said to be *racy*, and this zesty connotation soon raced forward to mean risqué.

- **requiem sharks**—Speaking of fish, white sharks are called *requiem sharks*, not because their killing of humans leads to so many funeral requiems, but because English mouths chewed up the French word for shark, *requin*, and spit it out as a word they knew, *requiem*. Talk about jaws!

- **school**—You can flunk the notion that a group of fish is called a *school* because fish swim together like kids in a school. Anyone who has seen groups of school kids knows fish are much more orderly in their travels. The fish type of school derives from the Old English *scolu*, meaning multitude. The education type of *school* comes from the Latin *schola*, meaning leisure devoted to learning.

- **sirloin**—When the story of a word's origin seems too good to be true, it probably isn't. *Sirloin*, for instance, actually derives from the French *surlonge* (over loin). But that meat and potatoes explanation can't compete with the one cooked up by the benighted people who claim a king liked this cut of beef so much he knighted it as "Sir Loin."

- **SOS**—The notion that the distress signal *SOS* (— •••—) is an acronym for "Save Our Ship" should be dashed. It's simply an easily memorized telegraphic sequence; dot's all.

- **ten-gallon hat**—The theory that a 10-gallon cowboy hat holds ten gallons of water doesn't hold water. It derives from the Mexican Spanish *sombrero galón*, for hat with braids, amigo.
- **waffle**—This word, meaning to waver has nothing to do with a breakfast food. While our word for a crisscrossed, baked battercake comes from the Dutch *wafel*, the *waffle* of our crisscrossing, half-baked politicians comes from *waff*, which means either to flutter or to yelp like a dog.
- **wing it**—Most people assume this term for ad libbing or improvising derives from the notion of doing something on the fly. In fact, it comes from theater, where an actor who "goes up" (forgets his lines) must depend on a prompter standing in the wings of the stage. In some cases, copies of the script are taped to curtains in the wings to help forgetful performers wing it.
- **worth your salt**—In Roman times, soldiers were paid in salt (*sal* in Latin), and that's why payment for work done is still called a *salary*. So you might assume the phrase "worth your salt" derives from these salty salaries.

  Nope. Here's the saline solution: "Worth your salt" comes from the salty beef, called *salt*, eaten by sailors. So a sailor who didn't perform his duties was said to be "not worth his salt."

Ornery Origins

Can you pick the correct origin of each word?

1) **pretzel**
   a) It's named for a New York City street vendor named "Zel," once known for his fanciful designs of a brittle biscuit baked in the shape of a loose knot; soon "a pretty Zel" was shortened to "a pretzel."

b) It's a German word derived from the Latin *bracchiatus* (having branches or arms) because a pretzel's shape resembles arms folded in prayer.

c) It's named for Pretsel, the misshapen little brother of Hansel and Gretel who appears in the original Grimms' fairy tale but not in its sanitized American version.

2) flamingo

a) It's named for Maria Flamingette, a 16th-century French aristocrat known for her long, beautiful neck.

b) It comes from *flam*, meaning a lie or hoax, as in *flim-flam*, because the flamingo pretends to be easy to catch but isn't.

c) It's derived from the Latin *flamma* (flame) because, upon taking flight, scarlet portions of the flamingo's wing, called *coverts* because they're usually hidden, flash into view like flame.

3) coupon

a) It's derived from the Latin *copula* (bond, pair), the same root that gives us *couple*, because the first coupons were always issued in pairs.

b) It comes from the Middle Dutch *kupe* (basket, tub), the same word that gives us *coop*, because merchants often placed coupons in tubs.

c) It's borrowed from the French *coup* (blow, stroke), the same root that gives us *coup d'etat*, because a coupon must be detached from a newspaper or flier with a blow or stroke.

4) bankrupt

a) It comes from the Italian *banca rotta* (broken bench). Early Italian bankers conducted their transactions on outdoor benches and when a banker became insolvent, his bench was all broken up (to say nothing of the banker himself).

b) It's a shortening of the expression "bank erupted!" used on the American frontier to describe a bank that collapsed during the financial panic of 1837.

c) It's named for George Bankrupt, a British banker who headed the Bank of London during its collapse in the 1740s.

Answers: 1) b 2) c 3) c 4) a

Chapter 4—

Write On!: Simple Secrets of Good Writing

People often assume the ability to write well is a God-given gift, a talent you either have or you don't.

Not true.

Great writers, like great ice skaters and musicians, become skillful through continual practice. Like athletes and performers, they must master the skills of their craft. Day in and day out, they write.

This chapter offers you several simple ways to improve your writing. Some are tips; some are tricks; and some are profound, esoteric secrets of the writing cult, revealed publicly here for the very first time.

Six handy tips

- **Vary the length of your sentences.**

  This may sound obvious, but few people realize the power you have when you follow a long sentence presenting complex ideas with a much shorter sentence that summarizes or emphasizes the point of the previous statements. Like a tennis player who lulls an opponent into complacency with leisurely ground strokes and then suddenly charges the net, a good writer occasionally inserts short sentences to drive the point home. Pow! It works.

- **Avoid long strings of prepositional phrases.**

  In most writing by average people in normal situations at work or at home on weekends or weekdays, people should avoid using several prepositional phrases in succession. As the previous sentence proves, they're tedious.

Prepositional phrases are like tiny barnacles that attach themselves one by one to the sleek hull of your ship-shape sentence. Before you know it, your sentence is weighed down by an accumulation of hangers *on*, or for that matter, hangers *off, at, in, of, over, by* and *on*, etc.

You can usually scrape off most prepositional barnacles by rewriting the sentence to include subordinate clauses or modifying phrases.

- **Transitions, transitions, transitions!**

Some regard these tiny words that connect one sentence to another as tinkerings, but don't leave these tinkerings, ever, to chance.

Like a house, a well-constructed essay or story includes doors and hallways that lead people easily and smoothly from one room to another. In prose, these passageways are supplied by transitions (terms like *these, that, such, for example, similarly* and *by contrast*) that make clear the relationship of each new idea to those that preceded it.

If such transitions are lacking, readers keep bumping into walls and opening closets trying to find their way from one idea to the next. But when transitions are included, your prose flows.

- **Balance the abstract and the concrete.**

Abstractions are as boring as a plain pizza. To give your writing zest, sprinkle the bland dough of generalization with specific details—tasty chunklets of pepper, onion and sausage.

William Shakespeare knew the magic of such morsels. When his character Hamlet, for instance, feels the cold cut of his mother's hasty remarriage, he speaks of cold cuts: "The funeral-baked meats did coldly furnish forth the marriage tables." Brrrrr.

- **Juxtapose contrasting images and ideas.**

  When Emily Dickinson wanted to convey the bittersweet emotions of leaving a loved one, she didn't write, "I have mixed feelings." She wrote, "Parting is all we know of heaven/And all we need of hell."

  This balancing of opposed words, called *antithesis*, can make the difference between night and day in your writing. Shakespeare knew it ("I come to bury Caesar, not to praise him"). So did 1960s anti-war protesters ("Make love, not war").

  At its best, antithesis attains the eloquence of Lincoln's "Gettysburg Address": "The world will little note nor long remember what we say here, but it can never forget what they did here."

- **End your sentences with punch.**

  I might have written, "Use punch to end your sentences." But the key word—*punch*—might have been lost.

  Sentences should build toward a peak. The sentence "After many hours, the climbers finally reached the peak" brings us to the top, while the sentence "The climbers finally reached the peak after many hours" lets us down.

Perilous Parallelism

"I like skiing and to ice skate, too."

"General Washington was first in war, first in peace and beloved by his countrymen."

"Superman pursued his never-ending crusade for truth, justice and the way we Americans live."

Although these sentences make sense, they also make scents—vague, indefinable aromas of awkwardness. One knows something is wrong with them, but it's hard to put one's nose on just what.

Here's what. They suffer from what linguists call "faulty parallelism," a diagnosis that sounds more like an error in geometry than in grammar. *"In geometry than in grammar"*—now there's a parallel phrase."

In essence, faulty parallelism is a failure to match substance and style. It occurs when two or more comparable items or ideas are presented using different grammatical structures. Whenever you sniff a whiff of faulty parallelism, you know the sentence writer has whiffed.

In the first sentence, for instance, "I like skiing and to ice skate, too," the noun "skiing" and the infinitive phrase "to ice skate" clash because they aren't parallel in structure. "I like skiing and ice skating too" glides much more smoothly over the grammatical glaze.

Likewise, although the second sentence may accurately describe our nonpareil president, Washington, it's not parallel. The lyrical rhythm established by "first in war" and "first in peace" is rudely interrupted by the unparallel phrase "beloved by his countrymen." Without the final parallelism of "first in the hearts of his countrymen," this sentence is a clown, not a classic.

Similarly, the geeky Clark Kent might fight for "truth, justice and the way we Americans live." But Superman, a guy from a truly parallel universe, crusades for "truth, justice and the American way."

Why worry about parallelism? After all, unparallel sentences may not be pretty, but they get their meaning across.

Not always.

Consider this sentence: "Some people like to eat corn as much as cattle." Because the parallelism in this sentence hasn't been made clear, it could mean either that people like to eat corn as much as cattle do, or that people like to eat corn as much as they like to eat cattle. (Believe me, to the cattle, this makes a big difference.) The parallelism can be clarified either by inserting "they do" before the word *cattle*, or inserting *do* after *cattle*.

Sometimes, parallelism is cleverly manipulated for humor, as the British did during World War II when they complained American soldiers were "overpaid, oversexed and over here." And occasionally you can violate parallelism for effect, as in "General Washington was first in war, first in peace and one heck of a guy."

But be careful. In generals and in general, it's a good idea to keep your skis, skates and phrases parallel.

E pluribus unity

If you want to write well, strive for unity in your paragraphs. Throughout history, the most mellifluous writers have been those with the discernment to craft paragraphs that leave a coherent and consolidated impression on the reader. In the future, I know I'll make sure each of my paragraphs is consistent in its audience, word choice, tense and tone.

Whoa!

That first paragraph is an extreme example of what can happen when writing lacks unity. While each sentence, taken by itself, is fairly clear, the overall impression is discordant and confusing. Reading it is like channel surfing from Martha Stewart to William F. Buckley to Mr. Rogers.

The first sentence, for instance, is authoritative, instructive and straightforward. It addresses the reader directly and informally ("you"), uses monosyllabic words, and cheers us on ("Come on, you can do it! To thine own paragraph be true!")

But the second sentence abruptly shifts direction. The tense has turned from the friendly present to the remote past ("throughout history," "have been"), and now the tone is ponderous, even pompous. Big words (*mellifluous, discernment*) float through it like gassy balloons in a Thanksgiving Day parade. You, the reader, are no longer the next-door neighbor ("you"), but the cloistered scholar at the end of the street (the third-person "reader").

Then, without warning, the whole scene changes again. Now we're suddenly in the first person ("I") and the future tense ("I'll try"). The writer affects a personal, New-Year's-resolution tone but uses just enough literary jargon (*audience, diction, tone*) to let us know who's boss.

By the end of this paragraph, after a whirlwind tour of moods, tenses, word choices and voices, we find ourselves be"whirl"dered and frustrated.

How can you prevent this from happening in your own writing?

In the same way that an artist selects a dominant tone, color, style or spatial pattern for each painting, you should choose an attitude, tense, audience and feel for each piece of writing, whether it's a minor memo or a mammoth masterpiece.

If you find yourself writing with a split personality, doctor your Jekyll and master your Hyde until you find that coherent, unified voice.

Give pace a chance

What's the difference between a sentence that sinks and a sentence that soars?

More often than not, the secret is beat.

As readers and listeners, we crave the natural rise and fall of sound. We love to hear the rolling surf of language crash, and subside…crash, and subside…crash, and subside. We want the rhythm of our phrases, like the English Channel waves in Matthew Arnold's poem "Dover Beach," to "begin, and cease, and then again begin."

Good writers reflect that natural cadence in the lift and lilt of their language. Notice, for instance, how Arnold carefully uses a pattern of an unstressed syllable followed by a stressed syllable to echo the sound of waves: "be-GIN and CEASE and THEN a-GAIN be-GIN."

If Arnold had changed one word—replaced the second *begin* with *start*, for instance—his wave-like rhythm would have been a wash: "beGIN and CEASE and THEN aGAIN START." Nope. Sounds clunky.

Professors call this short-long pattern an *iamb*, from the Greek word *iambos* (lame) because it resembles the halting gait of a person with a leg injury. Being more upbeat, I call it this the "heart-beat pattern" because it echoes the lub-dub of the human heart. (Like Popeye, "I amb what I amb.")

Another sailor, President John F. Kennedy, also understood the value of cadence. In his inaugural address, he assailed passivity with this sentence: "Ask NOT what your country can do for you." Like a good seaman, he secured his sentence with a tight *not*.

If he had begun that sentence with a less emphatic stress pattern, e.g., "Don't ask what your country can do for you," he would not have done as much for his country.

But you don't have to write a poem or an inaugural address to catch the beat. Sometimes the slightest adjustment in rhythm can pump up even a prosaic memo.

If you write to a subordinate, for instance, "I count on you to reach an agreement," your message may be muffled. That's because one word—*agreement*—destroys the iambic rhythm you've so carefully established in the first part of the sentence ("i COUNT on YOU to REACH an a-GREE-ment"). Instead of ending with a slam-dunk, your sentence dribbles out of bounds.

Instead, try using a word that sustains your hearty rhythm pattern—"I count on you to reach a deal." To paraphrase the anti-war protesters of the 1960s, all "I amb" saying is "give pace a chance."

Sentence, heal thyself!

The sentence doctor is in. Let's see if he can diagnose and cure these [sic] sentences taken from actual publications and essays. Say "aaaaah."

Patient: "Easterners moved out west and used their dominance to strip Native Americans of their land and livelihood to gain their own fortune and to boost their own power." **Diagnosis:** Sentence lacks focus because it's one long string of equally important verbs. **Remedy:** Use a subordinate clause and a participial phrase to turn some verbs into adjectives.

"Easterners, who moved out west to gain fortune and boost their own power, used their dominance to strip Native Americans of their land and livelihood."

Patient: "Our investors will not be able to avoid all stress, but, with our support, the experience for them could be less worrisome." **Diagnosis:** Wordy. Using two subjects ("investors," "experience") makes the sentence confusing. **Remedy:** Try subordinating one idea to the other. "Although we cannot eliminate all our investors' stress, our support can make their experience less worrisome."

Patient: "The causes for the Glorious Revolution are a crucial point of British history that historians should analyze in detail because these causes illustrate the foundation for British parliamentary power." **Diagnosis:** Flaws include passive verb ("are"), repetition ("history"/"historians"), and wordiness ("illustrate the foundation"). **Remedy:** "Historians should analyze in detail the reasons for the Glorious Revolution because those reasons shaped British parliamentary power."

Patient: "They didn't need to give him a lie detector test to have discovered his false claim of having passed the bar exam." **Diagnosis:** Wordy; becomes bogged down in complicated tenses ("have discovered," "having passed"). **Remedy:** "They could have discovered he lied about passing the bar exam without giving him a lie detector test."

Patient: "Leading up to the Civil War, there existed throughout the North an experience of difficult economic times and social turmoil." **Diagnosis:** The passive verb ("there existed") drains this sentence of punch. **Remedy:** "Before the Civil War, the North experienced difficult economic times and social turmoil."

Aaaaaaah.

Shoo that Wordy Wordpacker

In the category of annoyances, the vexatious practice of employing too many words to convey statement-making ideas is something that angers me to the extreme. Put simply, I hate wordiness.

As my first sentence suggests, that annoying pest Wordy Wordpacker can roost anywhere. He especially favors the florid foliage of letters written by job seekers who think prospective employers will be impressed by elaborate sentences and big words.

Let's see, for instance, if we can flush Wordy out of this sentence: "The characteristics of a job with Technical Enterprises Inc. that I find appealing include being able to make a difference toward the achievement of the protection of the environment."

Well, we know what the writer means…sort of. But tighten this sentence and make it a Titan. Forget "characteristics" and "include"; focus attention on the writer and the job: "A job with Technical Enterprises appeals to me because I'd be able to make a difference in protecting the environment." Or, if you really want to be Thoreau, simplify, simplify: "If I worked for Technical Enterprises, I could help protect the environment." That's telling 'em.

Here's another sentence that ranks high in the packing order: "My experiences with high-resolution lasers, on projects requiring knowledge of nuclear physics, and as a member of research teams investigating sunspots, were filled with dilemmas that demanded a quick and efficient response."

It's hard to believe the writer of this sentence could deliver a quick and efficient response to anything, but let's try to make his prose more efficient. Instead of having "experiences" being "filled," let's have the writer be skilled: "In my research on high-resolution lasers, nuclear physics and sunspots, I've solved dilemmas quickly and efficiently." Ah.

And now, the closer: "I am an individual who could actively contribute to the focus of an institution dedicated to doing vital research in my field."

Wordy, you nasty bird, get out of here! Shoo! Shoo! OK, let's try again: "I could help you perform vital research." That's better. When you're dealing with Wordy Wordpacker, if the "shoo" fits, pare it.

Tricky verbs can double you up

What's wrong with these sentences?:
"Our dog Pug is used to attack."
"We did film in Media 101 last year."
"In modeling school, we have studied poses."

As you probably noticed, the meaning of each sentence is ambiguous. That's because the verb phrase in each one ("is used," "did film" or "have studied") can be interpreted in two different ways.

The first sentence could mean either that Pug is accustomed to being attacked, or sent out to attack others. (If you're a mail carrier approaching Pug's house for the first time, there's a big difference.)

The second sentence could mean either that we studied film in Media 101 last year, or that we did, indeed, film something in that course. The third sentence could mean either that modeling students have learned about poses, or that they perform deliberate ("studied") poses.

What poses a problem with these three not-so-model sentences is that the verbs *use*, *did* and *have* can have two meanings.

Used can mean either familiar with ("get used to it"), or employed ("it's used like this"). *Did* is either a helping verb conveying emphasis ("you did know that"), or an action verb meaning to perform or accomplish ("you did it"). *Have* is either a helping verb indicating completed action ("you have learned this"), or an action verb meaning to possess or hold ("you have it now").

But by now you have had it and are wondering why I did do all this writing. Here's why: to warn you against using *used*, *did* and *have* as active verbs, especially in writing. To avoid confusion with their helping verb functions, replace *used*, *did* and *have* with action verbs that grip the pave"meant" more tightly.

Although I generally discourage replacing longer words with shorter ones, sometimes they're needed to make your meaning clear: "Our dog Pug is utilized (not "used") to attack." "We studied (not "did") film in "Media 101" last year." "In modeling school, we practice (not "have") studied poses."

Parallel parking with George

Can you tell what's wrong with each sentence in the following story about George, the nonpareil parker?

1) George spotted a parking space on a side street just wide enough for his car.

2) Abruptly stopping, he backed up.

3) He was skillful in driving, adept at using the clutch and had performed this maneuver many times.

4) Then suddenly, looking in the rear-view mirror, shock overwhelmed him.

5) He cursed the huge boat he was hauling behind him and his forgetfulness.

Answers:

1) As written, this sentence could mean either that the parking spot was just wide enough for George's car or that the street was just wide enough. Rewrite for clarity: "On a side street, George spotted a parking space just wide enough for his car."

2) A present participle (in this case "stopping") should be used to indicate *ongoing* action, not action that ceases before the action of the main verb. Because George can't stop the car and back it up at the

same time, rewrite the sentence to indicate consecutive action: "He stopped the car and backed it up."

3) George's parking may be parallel, but the elements of this sentence are not. The adjective phrases "skillful in driving" and "adept at using the clutch" should be followed by another adjective phrase, not the verb phrase "had performed this maneuver many times." Rewrite: "He was skillful in driving, adept at using the clutch and experienced in performing this maneuver."

4) "Looking in the rear-view mirror" is a misplaced participle, that is, an adjective ending in *ing* that seems to modify the wrong noun. As written, "looking in the rear-view mirror" describes "shock," which isn't something that can look in a rear-view mirror. Rewrite: "Looking in the rear-view mirror, George was overwhelmed with shock."

5) As written, this sentence could mean that George was hauling the boat behind his forgetfulness. Rewrite for clarity, either: "He cursed his forgetfulness and the huge boat he was hauling behind him," or "He cursed both the huge boat he was hauling behind him, and his own forgetfulness as well." Whatever floats your boat.

Chapter 5—

Bald Tires: Clichés, Jargon and Overused Terms

We need to be proactive, planful and focused in order to impact the bottom line. Unless we get with the program and actualize our parameters, we'll descend a slippery slope until we crash and burn.

Uggghhh!

Clichés and overused phrases like these are the bald tires of English. They've lost their traction—and their attraction. People who use such terms skid quickly off the road of clear communication.

To coin a phrase, "Enough is enough!"

Cliché—touché!

Asked to use the word *cliché* in a sentence, a student once wrote, "My father came home last night with a cliché on his face." When his teacher asked him what he meant, the student explained that the dictionary defined *cliché* as a tired, worn out expression.

Unfortunately, too many of our sentences also come home with clichés on their faces. Thinking writing is as "easy as pie," we're afraid to "go out on a limb" and to "push the envelope." Instead, we stick with the "tried and true," using "garden-variety" phrases that "bore people to tears."

Sometimes we pack so many clichés into one sentence that their metaphoric meanings clash like "oil and water." That's what happened to the book reviewer who wrote: "Then a sleazy journalist with a bone to pick with Bop uses his poison pen to wreak as much havoc as possible."

And sometimes clichés become so familiar that we overlook their double meanings, as this student did: "The sonnet says that, since the man is about to die, the girl should love him up to the hilt."

Because journalists often cover the same stories day in and "daze" out, they're particularly prone to clichés. In their stories, coups are always "bloody," effects are always "chilling," downturns are always "steep," optimism is always "cautious" and increases are always "whopping."

Believe it or not, tired phrases such as "wake-up call," "ballpark figure" and "take the bull by the horns" were once fresh and original. But now, like aging child movie stars, they aren't so cute any more.

So why do we keep using clichés? Mostly because it's so easy. Banal phrases are the handy nickels, dimes and quarters of English, always jingling in our pockets. We insert them into the vending machines of our prose and—presto!—we get a predictable response from our readers.

But, unfortunately, all we usually get from a vending machine is junk food—cheap, packaged confections and snacks offering little nutrition or flavor. Clichés will never elicit the freshness, complexity and zest of a delicacy prepared by a four-star chef.

So here's a four-star generalization: When you find yourself using a cliché in your writing, ask why. Is it laziness, lack of creativity or, as is often the case, imprecision about what you're trying to say? When it comes to clichés, more is less.

Mallonics, bizonics and TVonics

When the Oakland, Calif., school board passed a resolution declaring Black English (or Ebonics) a second language, I couldn't help imagining how discussions of this issue might sound in three other "second languages": "mallonics" (the language of suburban teenagers), "bizonics" (the language of corporate managers) and "TVonics" (the language of TV newscasters)…

Mallonic #1: When I heard they, like, wanna, like, call Black English, like, a second language, I was all, like, whoa!

Mallonic #2: Me too. I was, like, that's so random! Get a life!

Mallonic #1: When I told my friend, she goes, "That's sooo not fair." And then I go, "I mean, like, if people can't, like, speak English right, they should, like, get a grip or something, you know?" It's really, like, way bogus, ya' know?

Mallonic #2: Whatever.

* * * * * * * *

Bizonic #1: This recent repositioning of the diversity-enhanced linguistic infrastructure has negatively impacted our evaluation assessment adjustment mode.

Bizonic #2: I agree. How can you actualize bottom-line accountability with a skills-mix adjustment pool comprised of a grammatically deficient human resources sector?

Bizonic #1: We might have to outsource a Bizonics Implementation Specialist to reengineer our syntactic compliance paradigm.

Bizonic #2: You're right; otherwise we'll have to surplus human resource assets to maximize the cost savings in our force management reduction program.

* * * * * * * *

TVonic #1: In a wake-up call for educators across the nation, the Oakland school board has started down the slippery slope to a bizarre and tragic development.

TVonic #2: You're right. In trying to level the playing field, Oakland has jump-started the heated debate over a political football.

TVonic #1: Yes, their hard-line stance has unleashed a firestorm of criticism that could spark a chilling effect and trigger a steep downturn.

TVonic #2: Perhaps they'll hammer out an 11th-hour agreement that sends a very clear signal to other embattled and strife-torn school boards at this defining moment.

TVonic #1: We can only hope so.

Arguing with arguably

The word *arguably* is arguably the favorite refuge of the habitual hedger. It's especially popular among those courageous reporters and commentators who want to say something superlative but fear committing themselves to absolute statements. Because their quivers lack the arrows of expert qualifications, they quiver in qualification.

Consider these highly qualified assessments of people who are highly qualified: "[Alfred Stieglitz] became arguably the first photographer to translate the artless brashness of New York into conscious art." "Lou Gehrig is arguably one of the very best baseball players ever to play."

What's next? "George Washington was arguably the first President of the United States"?

Arguably is now so overused that I keep imagining someone listening to today's radio news reports asking, "Who is this guy R. Gube Lee who keeps popping up like Forrest Gump in every story? It's always, 'R. Gube Lee, Al Gore and George W. Bush are the front runners,' or, 'He is R. Gube Lee, one of the most powerful figures in Washington.'"

Oddly enough, while the adverb *arguably* is almost always used in a positive sense, suggesting that the statement being argued is true, its adjective form, *arguable*, can bear the connotation of either surety or doubt. For instance, if we say that an action's legality is arguable, we could mean either that it's questionable or that it's legitimate.

In this sense, *arguable* is a lot like the adjective *moot*, which can mean either debatable ("that's a moot question"), or not debatable ("that's a moot point.")

Meanwhile, back at the rant…Is *arguably* over used? Arguably, yes. Let's lift our glasses and milquetoast *arguably* as the wishy-washy word of the 2000s.

Little shop of horrors

Have you noticed that every ordinary retail store is now a "center"? In my neighborhood, for instance, the Puppy Center does its business, so to speak, near the Quick Print Center, which copies the name of the Arrow Prescription Center across the street. Perhaps, in addition to The National Centers for Disease Control, we need a National Centers for *Center* Control.

Meanwhile, business can't seem to get *system* out of its system. People don't buy shampoo any more; they buy a "hair-care system," replete with washes, rinses, and conditioners. When I needed some bookshelves, someone tried to sell me an elaborate "wall system." "I'm just storing my books," I told him, "not trying to keep out barbarian invaders."

We've also been victimized by *kit* kitsch. While searching for some salad dressing in the supermarket the other day, I came upon the Et Tu Caesar Salad Kit, containing dressing, cheese, croutons, bacon-flavored bits but, unfortunately, no caboodle. I wonder if, during Julius Caesar's salad days as a commander in Gaul, his legions carried regular mess kits or, in a weird premonition of their leader's assassination, Et Tu Caesar Salad Kits.

Add *collection* to this inflationary collection. From reading the package of Pepperidge Farm's Nantucket chocolate chip cookies, for instance, I learn these are no ordinary cookies; they're part of Pepperidge Farm's

American Collection, a line that includes other offerings like Chesapeake, Tahoe and Sausalito.

I wonder whether this collection is displayed in a special gallery at the Museum of Modern Art (perhaps near Cézanne's pears), or whether I'm going to turn on the TV some day and see high-fashion models in cookie bags striding down runways as Pepperidge Farm unveils its new autumn collection. (I hear some of those models are tough cookies.)

Surfacing edgy clichés

- **frame**—This is today's trendy substitute for *control* or *shape*. Democrats worry, for instance, that Republicans will frame the debate on campaign finance reform, that is, determine its limits, structure and content.

- **revisit**—No one returns to or reconsiders a subject any more; he or she revisits it, as in "let's revisit campaign finance reform." (Let's not.) For some reason, when I hear the word *revisit*, I always picture Victorian visitors in bonnets and top hats prancing into someone's parlor (twice!) on a Sunday afternoon. (By the way, didn't you always hate it when your elementary school teacher described classroom talking as "visiting with your neighbors"?)

- **surface**—As long as we're surfacing trendy words, how about *surface*? I don't mind a submarine's surfacing or even someone's surfacing my driveway, but now everyone is surfacing (exposing or identifying) problems and issues.

- **situation**—Here's the *situation* situation: everyone is adding the redundant *situation* to words and phrases. I recently heard someone describe a batch of resignations as "resignation situations."

  TV news programs have become *situation* comedies. TV newscasters always tack on the word *situation* to whatever they talk about—the "weather situation," the "crime situation," etc., instead of saying simply "weather" or "crime."

- **Show me the money!**—A couple of years ago, this catchphrase from the popular movie *Jerry Maguire* was well on its way to becoming one of the most overused American terms of all times. For a while, it ranked right up there with "Sock it to me!" from the 1960s and "Where's the beef?" from the 1980s. It was everywhere.

But then something incredible happened. In their mighty linguistic wisdom, the American people suddenly realized that the phrase with attitude had become a platitude.

So they dropped it. Just like that. Soon it was a dead mantra walking.

- **obscene**—This word, which originally denoted depravity or indecency, is now *de rigueur* in any description of large monetary sums. Show them the money and you're sure to hear about "obscene profits," "obscene salaries" and "obscene prices."

- **icon**—Icon is the little cliché that could, huffing and puffing its way up a "slippery slope," all the while chanting, "I think icon, I think icon."

- **soccer moms**—Political pundits get a real kick out of this term. It refers to harried, SUV-driving suburban moms whose main sideline is standing on the sidelines of their kids' soccer games.

- **basically**—Basically, the problem is, basically, that some people basically overuse this word. Well, at least it's replacing the overworked term "bottom line."

- **in terms of**—In terms of overuse, "in terms of" should be terminated.

- **redemptive**—If I read one more newspaper or magazine review describing a novel as "redemptive," I'm going to return to the newsstand and demand a redemption. OK, so a lot of novels tell stories of recovery or salvation, but their reviewers should pray for a word more imaginative than *redemption* to describe it.

- **looking to**—Have you noticed that no one "expects to," "hopes to" or "seeks to" do something any more? These days, everyone is "looking to" relocate, "looking to" get a promotion, "looking to" win a game. Imagine a 1990s version of the U.S. Constitution: "We the people of the United States, looking to form a more perfect union…" Ugh!

- **edgy**—When people use *edgy* these days, they usually don't mean nervous or irritable; they mean having a sharp or biting edge. Any film, book or song that breaks new ground is now described as *edgy*. A recent magazine piece, for instance, hailed an innovative project as "creative, edgy, saucy." Personally, I like *edgy*, with its connotation of pushing things to the edge, but its overuse makes me edgy.

- **marquee matchup**—In sports, every big game or bout is now heralded as a "marquee matchup," presumably because such contests are featured on the marquees of the arenas or stadiums in which they occur. It's catching. In class the other day, I found myself describing the Lincoln-Douglas debates as a "marquee matchup." How about de Lafayette vs. de Sade? Now that would be a true marquis matchup.

- **in a heartbeat**—Taking the pulse of American language, I've discovered that nothing is done in a flash or in a second anymore. It's done "in a heartbeat." The phrase pumps out a nice blend of emotion and urgency, and maybe that's why people often use it to express their hearts' desires: "If I won the lottery, I'd quit this job in a heartbeat." But overuse has brought fibrillation. It may be time to make a cardiac arrest.

- **effortful, impactful, planful**—You don't need a Fulbright to notice that the suffix -*ful* is attaching itself like a lamprey to many nouns. While this practice apparently brings fulfillment to bureaucrats, psychobabblers and full professors, it brings a full-fledged fulmination to my throat. Be "cautionful," "wisdomful" and "discretionful"; put a full nelson on this suffix.

Leveling the battlefield

You remember Abraham Lincoln's "Gettysburg Address," the one that begins "Four score and seven years ago," that celebrates the sacrifice of "brave men, living and dead," and calls for a "new birth of freedom"? Some historians consider it the greatest speech ever made by an American.

Re-reading Lincoln's address recently, I couldn't help wondering what this eloquent masterpiece would have sounded like had it been delivered in the business jargon and obfuscatory bureaucratese of public pronouncements today…

Within the parameters of an 87-year time period, our progenitors engendered on the Atlantic Rim, a state-of-the-art political paradigm, prioritized in personal empowerment, with an up-front sign-off on the mandate of a level playing field.

At this point in time, we are engaged in "Operation Just Fratricide," testing whether that paradigm, or any paradigm so prioritized, can achieve sustainability. We are met on a level playing field of that intra-ethnic conflict with a breakaway republic. We have come to resource a statistically significant percentage of that field as a final destination for those who have been terminally outplaced so that this paradigm might be ongoing for the foreseeable future.

But, taking the long view, we can not resource—we cannot access—we cannot impact—this ground. The cowardice-challenged personnel, operative and inoperative, who competed in this arena, have arguably impacted it far above our modalities to enhance or disenhance. The family of nations will be out of the loop about our dialogue here, but it will always have a great comfort level with what they did here.

It is for us the viable, rather, to sign on to the long-range plan, which those who pushed the envelope here have thus far formulated. Our mandate is to actualize the great agenda on our plate—that from these honored outplaced we take enhanced commitment to the priorities they opted for—that we buy into the notion that these outplaced shall not have been derecruited in vain, that this entity, under Top Management, shall have a revitalization of discretionary activity—and that governmental systems of the average, middle-class American families, by the average middle-class American families, for the average middle-class American families, shall not be zeroed out in the new world order.

A senseless tragedy gone terribly wrong

Flash! Here's the latest news bulletin from the JCN (Journalistic Cliché News Service):

Amid mounting calls for his resignation, self-styled language kingpin Rob Kyff, arguably the nation's top foe of journalese, lashed out at the cliché-ridden writing style he claims is stalking our newsrooms. For the past seven years, seasoned media observers, headquartered in a sprawling installation near a remote mountain outpost, have conducted 11th-hour marathon talks in a last-ditch effort to avert a showdown with the grammar guru.

Meanwhile, speaking about the all-important language issue before a group of largely partisan supporters, the embattled Kyff vehemently denied allegations that his proposed measures will lead to downsizing in American newsrooms.

"We still need reporters," he said, "who can pack tired phrases such as 'amid mounting calls,' 'skyrocketing costs,' 'last-ditch effort,' '11th-hour marathon talks,' 'sprawling installations,' 'avert a showdown,' and 'vehemently denied' into their stories. We even need those who can weave hackneyed constructions such as 'many of them,' 'what was once,' 'in what some are calling,' and 'has become a Mecca' into their stories."

Kyff's supporters, many of them wiping away tears, stood in the bombed-out building that was once his office, an office that has become a Mecca for tourists and souvenir hunters. In what some are calling a key political benchmark, Kyff targeted broadcast journalists. "You TV reporters and anchors, with your cliché-ridden bathos, are the worst," he said.

Asked for a reaction to Kyff's attack, local TV reporter John Blowdried said, "Joy turned to sorrow today, as this tragic turn of events unfolded. This personal attack on an entire industry is not only a disturbing development but a brutal and senseless tragedy. It's a shocking tale of lies, drugs and murder, of shallow, unmarked graves in remote wooded areas, of love gone suddenly and terribly wrong.

"In the wake of this disaster," Blowdried continued, "we in television are picking through the rubble of our lives, trying to sort it all out, trying to make sense of a senseless tragedy. Frankly, our newsroom looks like a war zone, and onlookers can only look on in silent horror.

"In a related development," Blowdried added, "Kyff's neighbors described him as a quiet man, who kept largely to himself."

Poetic justice

Listen my readers and you shall hear

Some terms I've really come to fear:

Closure, enabling, proactive and *phat*;

Show me the money! We've been there, done that.

Paradigm shifts we'd sure like to sever,

With *arguably, road rage, designer—whatever.*

Defining moment and *slippery slope*

Are *literally pushing the envelope.*

In terms of clichés, *in terms of* should go;

Stay *focused, cost-conscious, empowered, ya' know?*

With *soccer moms, sales events—Please don't go there;*

At the end of the day, it's *your worst nightmare.*

Regarding *parameters* we really know nada;

And *cyber-space* jargon is just *yadda, yadda.*

On televised news, all *perps* are *shot dead*

In *exclusive* reports we, *like, totally* dread.

Bizarre *home invasions* are telecast live,

While *late-breaking* stories invariably thrive.

It's always a *standoff* or *situation,*

While *global warming* kills civilization.

Where *basically* buzzwords do frolic and revel

On *playing fields* always so perfectly *level.*

Chilling effects and *wake-up calls*—Tsk!—

Are always *impacting* those children *at risk.*

Where *break-out* albums by *pop icons* wail,

And suffixes *-driven* and *-wise* have grown stale.

And no, *this isn't about you, okay?*

Revisit that issue on some other day.

And while we're *on hold*, they really don't woo us

By saying, *Your call is important to us.*

And finally we access the real *bottom line* -

The most annoying cliché of our time.

No longer do people say *yeah, ya* or *yes*;

It's now *absolutely*—please *give it a rest!*

Quizzical Expressions

Can you decipher these well-known maxims that have been translated into bureaucratic gobbledygook? This may seem like an impossible task, but remember, where there is sufficient positive volition, a method of achieving an objective can be determined. ("Where there's a will, there's a way.")

1) The warm-blooded, feathered, egg-laying vertebrate animal that arrives at a venue first invariably comes into possession of a small, legless, invertebrate, crawling animal.

2) Decipher the folds of flesh surrounding my mouth: no nascent revenue enhancements.

3) Everything that coruscates with effulgence is not *ipso facto* auriferous.

4) A short vocal utterance directed toward individuals possessing a high degree of knowledge meets adequately all the needs of the occasion.

5) A small polished steel instrument used at the appropriate chronological moment is tantamount to saving the square root of 81.

6) When residing in the capital of Italy and its environs, be certain to assume a behavioral manner akin to the permanent inhabitants of the aforementioned geographical location.

7) Every cumulus accumulation of hydrogen oxide vapor possesses a radiant inner structure.

8) Do not become lachrymose because of the accidental overturning of a receptacle containing a white, lactose-rich, nutritive substance.

9) A giftee would be wise to abolish the habitual casting of glances into the oral cavity of equestrian specimens.

10) If you verbalize the discourse, it's imperative that you perambulate the pedestrian journey.

Translations:

1) The early bird gets the worm.

2) Read my lips: no new taxes.

3) All that glitters is not gold.

4) A word to the wise is sufficient.

5) A stitch in times saves nine.

6) When in Rome, do as the Romans do.

7) Every cloud has a silver lining.

8) Don't cry over spilled milk.

9) Don't look a gift horse in the mouth.

10) If you talk the talk, you gotta walk the walk.

Chapter 6—

Comma Knowledge:
The Perils of Punctuation

Punctuation leaves many of us "comma"tose. Apostrophe catastrophes make us hyphenventilate, while quotation marks send us into a mad dash. And many of us simply hate punctuation. Period.

But punctuation is important. Just ask Angela Penfold.

Penfold lost her job as a nurse at a British health center when she wrote top officials to complain about her supervisor. Her letter contained this fateful sentence: "I have come to the opinion Mrs. Pepperell is out to make my life hell, so I give in my notice."

Because of the comma following *hell*, officials thought Penfold was quitting. But that's not what she intended. "I just meant that she was trying to get me to hand in my notice," Penfold said.

Oops!

Good ol' comma sense

- **comma pile ups**

   When it comes to using commas, we're all comma criminals; none of us can avoid making errors involving these frustrating, difficult, pesky little devils.

   Speaking of which, shouldn't there be a comma after *pesky?*

   Devilishly good question.

   When two adjectives in a series of adjectives are equal in their relationship to the noun they modify, they're called "coordinate adjectives," and you should insert commas between them. Thus, if we omitted the word *little*, we'd write, "those difficult, frustrating, pesky devils," inserting commas after each adjective except the last.

In these cases, commas function like the hands of football officials who reach into the pile-up after a fumble to sort out the players (adjectives) and see who has the football (noun).

A good test of whether adjectives are coordinate is to see whether you can insert *and* between them, then reverse them and still have the sentence make sense. So, because we could write "those pesky and frustrating and difficult commas," the adjectives are coordinate, and the commas between the adjectives are necessary.

But what happens when we want to talk about those "frustrating, difficult, pesky *little* devils?"

In this case, *little* forms a satanic blood pact with the noun *devils*, in the same way a player in the pile-up who grabs the football forms an unshakable bond with it. So "little devils," like the player and his treasured football, are thought of as a unit, as opposed to "big devils" or "medium-sized devils." Because we really don't mean "those little and pesky devils," the comma after *pesky* can be dropped.

Generally, when an adjective forms such a compound with a noun and the two words are thought of as a single item, you can drop the comma after a preceding adjective.

Thus, "those lazy, hazy, crazy days of summer" (not "those lazy hazy crazy days of summer") are perfect for "pastoral, languid baseball" (not "pastoral languid baseball"). But a "cool September day" (not "a cool, September day") is perfect for "an exciting football game" (not "an exciting, football game").

Now it's your turn to drive. See whether you can place the commas properly in these adjective phrases:

1) a dark blue wool suit

2) an expensive tree-lined regulation tennis court

3) a sturdy tall tree

4) a sturdy strong maple tree

5) a sturdy sugar maple tree

6) a thoughtful considerate intelligent teacher

7) a warm appealing good humor

8) large wooden kitchen cabinets

Answers:

1) a dark blue wool suit

2) an expensive, tree-lined regulation tennis court

3) a sturdy, tall tree

4) a sturdy, strong maple tree

5) a sturdy sugar maple tree

6) a thoughtful, considerate, intelligent teacher

7) a warm, appealing good humor

8) large wooden kitchen cabinets.

- **Crunching those serial commas**

Would you pop in a comma after *Crackle* in this sentence? "I like Snap, Crackle and Pop."

If so, you're a putter-inner. If not, you're a leaver-outer.

Putter-inners heed "comma" sense. They're cautious, precise and darn good accountants. Leaver-outers read the "Comma" Sutra. They're spontaneous, carefree and darn good kissers.

While Al Gore, Martha Stewart and Miss Manners are putter-inners, Jim Carrey, Howard Stern and Madonna are leaver-outers.

That comma before the *and* in a series of items is called "a serial comma" (or, in the case of "Snap, Crackle, and Pop," a "cereal comma.")

Believe it or not, this Rice Krispie-shaped object has broken up everything from law firms to rock groups. Look at Crosby, Stills,

Nash and Young," or as Nash and Young preferred it, "Crosby, Stills, Nash, and Young."

And where do our language experts, those unwavering arbiters of decisiveness and authority, stand on the serial comma issue?

They disagree.

Some say inserting a serial comma before *and* is redundant. Most newspapers and magazines omit serial commas, but for a much more profound and esoteric reason: it saves ink. Other authorities say serial commas avoid confusion in sentences such as these:

"Their breakfast included orange juice, coffee, much talk of commas and cereal." (Insert a comma after *commas* and it's clear they were eating cereal, not talking about it.)

"Tom had two kinds of breakfast food, Rice Krispies and Cheerios." (Insert a comma after "Rice Krispies" and it's clear Tom had two kinds of breakfast food, not four.)

"Tina ordered bacon, eggs, coffee with sugar and milk." (Insert a comma after *sugar* and it's clear Tina had coffee with sugar and also had a glass of milk.)

"Breakfast cereals can be classified into these categories: sugarcoated, fruited, unsweetened and whole-grained. (Insert a comma after *unsweetened*, and it's clear there are four categories, not three.)

Here's my snap judgment: if you want your sentences to crackle with clarity, pop in a serial comma.

One danger of omitting a serial comma is illustrated in this phrase about baseball manager Felipe Alou: "Alou, whose lineup included Marquis Grissom, Larry Walker, Ken Hill and his son, Moises..." Because there's no serial comma after "Ken Hill," the reader would assume the son is his, when in fact it's Felipe's.

Likewise, this passage shows how a serial comma can make a big difference in meaning: "…how men and women work and play, raise their children, worship their gods, live and die."

The absence of a comma after *live* raises the question (as opposed to the children) of whether the writer was thinking of "live and die" as one activity, or two separate activities.

Speaking of living and dying, here's a comma folk tale to die for: A man's will stipulated that his estate be given to "John, Mary and Alice." On the basis of the absence of a serial comma after *Mary*, John argued that the estate should be divided into two parts, half for him and half for Mary and Alice.

The case went to court and the greedy John won, clearly proving that all of gall is divided into two, not three parts.

- **Comma-kazis**

   On the highway of English, commas are flashing yellow lights. They tell the reader to slow down, look around, beware. Omit a comma at a dangerous linguistic intersection and your phrases can collide— often with disastrous results. Look what happens, for instance, to our hapless crash dummy, Uncle George, when commas are omitted from these sentences:

   "While Jane barbecues Uncle George can shuck the corn." Ouch!

   "If you drive over Uncle George won't be home." Splat!

   Insert commas after *barbecue* in the first sentence and after *over* in the second, and Uncle George is no longer being barbecued or driven over. Phew!

   Now try untangling these linguistic collisions by inserting a well-placed comma:

   1) Jane cheered hard for her team had scored.

   2) The cold wind blew the snow fell and the lake froze.

3) The babysitter agreed to look after the children had left the house.

4) Those first-graders who can read several stories a day.

5) I went to the ball game with Tom and Jane and Uncle George watched it on TV.

Solutions:

1) Insert a comma after *hard*. (*For* means the same thing as *because*)

2) Insert a comma after *blew*.

3) Insert a comma after *look*. (She agreed to look for something lost.)

4) Insert a comma after *can*.

5) If Jane went to the game, insert a comma after *Jane*; if she watched it on TV, insert a comma after *Tom*.

Shake hands with a hyphen

When two words come together, they often affirm their friendly meeting with a hyphen-handshake.

Unfortunately, we're often as unsure about hyphens as we are about handshakes. Do we shake hands, for instance, with our girl-friend? (Nope. It's *girlfriend*.) With our half-brother? (Nope. It's *half brother*.) With our great-aunt? (Yup. It's *great-aunt*.)

When you're in doubt about compound words and handshakes like these, it's best to consult a dictionary (and your great-aunt's will).

But what really cause us to "hyphen-ventilate" are questions involving compound adjectives. Is it "thinly veiled threat" or "thinly-veiled threat"? "Much admired writer" or "much-admired writer"? Here's a handy guide to what's shakin':

- **a friendly old rule:** If each of the two adjacent adjectives could modify the noun separately, omit the hyphen: "the friendly old dog," "eager young faces."
- **a much-observed rule that's much observed:** When two words forming a compound adjective *precede* a noun, use a hyphen. But when two words forming a compound adjective *follow* a noun, generally omit the hyphen. Thus, "The well-played game was well played," and, "The tough-minded executive was tough minded."
- **a very much followed, highly regarded and most respected rule:** Even when a compound adjective precedes a noun, don't use a hyphen when: 1) "very" is added to it ("a very well played game"); 2) one of the two words is an adverb ending in -*ly* ("a safely played game"); 3) one of the words is *most, least* or *less* ("the most talented player," "the least qualified candidate").
- **A little-heeded rule that's not a little heeded one:** Insert or omit hyphens carefully to avoid ambiguity. A little-washed shirt, for instance, may be dirtier than a little washed shirt. An ill-clothed baby may be healthier than an ill clothed baby. A light-blue backpack may be heavier than a light blue backpack.
- **A rule that's all-knowing and self-fulfilling:** Even when a compound adjective follows a noun, use a hyphen when one of the combining words is *all* or *self* (except for *selfless* and *selfsame*): "God is all-knowing, self-confident and selfless, and even this selfsame Deity has problems with hyphens."

Rural plurals and other apostrophe catastrophes

Apostrophes.

Ya' can't live with 'em, and you cannot live without them.

On the one hand, more and more people seem to be inserting unnecessary apostrophes at the end of plural words. This seems to be most common on hand-lettered roadside signs ("Apple's for Sale," "Free Kitten's," "Auto Repair's").

Some say this practice may have started with the use of the implied possessive on mailboxes. *The Smiths'* on a mailbox, for instance, would technically be correct because it's a shortened version of "The Smiths' home."

Whatever its origin, this down home "rural plural" is becoming citified fast. The ever-vigilant Merriam-Webster's Dictionary of English Usage, for instance, has even recorded these uses in respectable publications: "the buyback's included Texaco's purchase"; "(equestrian) judge's look for"; "the finest Tibetan Mastiff's."

On the other hand, more and more people seem to be *omitting* the apostrophe from the contraction of "it is."

"YES ITS TRUE," blared a recent classified ad for an unfurnished apartment (heat, hot water and apostrophe presumably not included). Meanwhile, a newspaper article about film credits rendered a spoken quotation this way: "I don't want to list a greensman if its not a jungle picture."

Believe it or not, grammarians have been griping about rural plurals since 1770 when Robert Baker condemned the plurals *idea's*, *opera's* and *virtuoso's*.

And people have been confusing the contraction *it's* with the genitive *its* for centuries. In fact, just two hundred years ago, *it's* was more common than *its* as the possessive form of *it*. "Estimate it's merit," wrote Thomas Jefferson in 1787.

So before using an apostrophe, take Jefferson's advice. Estimate its merit to avoid an apostrophe catastrophe.

Dating in the 2000s

You might call it the punctuation controversy of the new century—whether to write *2000's* with an apostrophe or without (*2000s*). *The New York Times,* for instance, uses *2000's*, while most other publications favor *2000s*. Like the apostrophe itself, we readers feel caught in the middle.

This controversy goes back several decades. Way back in the 1990s/1990's, Tim Everett, a student at the University of Connecticut law school, reported that he saw *1990's* more often than *1990s* and wondered whether the apostrophe might be inserted for aesthetic reasons. "Does it act," he asked, "as a visual bridge, a sort of elision between two orthographic modes, the Arabic numeral zero and the letter *s*?"

But others ask, if *2000's* is not possessive, why the apostrophe?

Why indeed? Traditionally, apostrophes have always been added to form the plurals of letters, numerals, symbols, and words referred to as words. Thus, a pro football coach draws *x's* and *o's*, tries to put *6's* on the scoreboard, makes big *$'s* and abides no *if's*, *and's* or *but's* from his players.

But (sorry, Coach) many grammatical experts have declared apostrophes in plural numbers to be superfluous. "The *1890's* is an unnecessary use of the apostrophe," decrees Edward D. Johnson in *The Handbook of Good English*. "The plural number is just as clear without it."

Still, I rather like Mr. Everett's poetic explanation—that the apostrophe, like a grammatical Brooklyn Bridge, spans the gap between numbers and letters, carrying the reader smoothly from numerical to alphabetical shores. But then again, I might be accused of trying to sell you the Brooklyn Bridge.

So, to quote the instructions on a friend's answering machine: "This is the 2000s; you know what to do."

And I quote...

Quotation marks are like belly buttons. When they're near other punctuation marks (commas, question marks, colons, periods, etc.), we have only one question about them: "Are they innies or outies?" In other words, do the quotation marks go inside or outside the adjacent punctuation marks?

To avoid "navel" warfare, let's belly up to this quiz. Should the closing quotation marks in each case be innies or outies?

1) The economist Quarrel Marks once told his comrades, "Give a man a punctuation mark and you feed him for a day; teach a man to punctuate and you're fed up with him every day".

2) "Comrades who use hyphens", Marks once declared, "will surely dash to higher income brackets."

3) Marks said, "The colon is attached to the navel;" that's what he said.

4) Attempting to "train" his comrades, Marks provided a list of what he called "punk-choo-choo-ation": commas, hyphens, apostrophes and periods.

5) Marks once asked, "If I'm found guilty of breaking a punctuation law, will I get a long sentence"?

6) Did Marks say, "Punctuators of the world unite; you have nothing to lose but your brains?"

7) Did Marks ask, "If my comrades are well trained in punctuation, will they run a punctual train?"?

Answers:

1) "…day." Always place periods inside closing quotation marks.

2) "…hyphens," Always place commas inside closing quotation marks.

3) "…navel"; Always place semicolons outside closing quotation marks.

4) "…-ation": Always place colons outside closing quotation marks.

5) "…sentence?" If the question mark applies only to the quoted question, place it inside the quotation marks.

6) "…brains"? If the question mark applies to the entire sentence, place it outside the quotation marks.

7) "…punctual train?" Use no more than one end mark at the end of a quotation, even if the second question mark applies to the entire sentence.

Dot's her!

A fierce debate has been raging in my school's English department over whether the courtesy title *Ms.* should be followed by a period.

No, say the "Ms"-creants. They argue that, since *Ms* is an invented word and not an abbreviation for anything, it doesn't need a period. While *Mr.* stands for *Mister* and *Mrs.* stands for *Mistress*, they say, *Ms.* doesn't stand for anything, and they simply won't stand for its having a period.

Yes, say the "Ms."-behavers, a generally docile caucus of scholars who occasionally lift their heads from grading term papers just long enough to mumble something about *Ms* without a period "looking funny."

The *Ms./Ms* issue, which, by the way, crosses gender and generational lines, pops up, well, periodically. Seeking to end this "Ms."-ery once and for all, I consulted *The New York Public Library Writer's Guide to Style and Usage* and found this: "Technically, *Ms.* should not have a period because it is not an abbreviation, but the period is there nonetheless for consistency and equivalency to *Mr.*" Period.

Though this seemed to solve the "Ms."-tery, I was left wondering why *Miss*, which, like *Mrs.*, is an abbreviation for *Mistress*, has no period. Shouldn't the rule of consistency and equivalency apply here too? Or is it just hit or "Miss"?

Leaving the Messrs., Mmes., Mses., Misses and messes of the English department behind, I wondered over to a history department meeting where several bespectacled colleagues were debating the use of a period following the *S* in Harry S Truman's name. "Truman's middle name was simply *S*," one teacher was arguing, "so *S* isn't an abbreviation for anything."

Donning a skin-tight shirt with a large *S* (no period) on the chest, I jumped into a phone booth and once again accessed *The New York Public Library Writer's Guide to Style and Usage*. It reported that, although history books generally include Truman's period (1945-1953), they usually omit his period. But the entry was careful to note that Truman himself inserted a period "when he thought of it."

As Harry used to say, "if you can't stand periodic ambiguity, get out of the kitchen."

Comma Suture

Where would you insert or delete commas in these sentences?:

1) Punctuation is a window on the soul but it's not the sole window.
2) Commas can chop up sentences, and slow down readers.
3) Like counting pennies counting other people's commas can leave you "comma"-tose.
4) Some books include comma rules, devised during the 19th century.
5) Don't insert a comma, unless it's necessary.
6) A punctuation mark that's seemingly innocuous, casual and unimportant can actually make a big difference.
7) Robert Frost's first book of poems *A Boy's Will* contains many commas.
8) Robert Frost's book of poems, *A Boy's Will,* contains many commas.

Answers:

1) comma after *soul* (Use a comma before a word joining two independent clauses: "punctuation is" and "it's not.")
2) no comma after *and* ("And slow down readers" is not an independent clause, so no comma is needed before it.)
3) comma after *pennies* (Use a comma after an introductory word group.)
4) no comma after *rules* ("Devised during the 19th century" is restrictive; it tells which rules.)
5) no comma after *comma* ("Unless you're sure it's necessary" is essential, not parenthetical, to the meaning of the sentence.)
6) no comma after *unimportant* (Don't use a comma after the last item in a series.)

7) commas before and after *A Boy's Will* (The word *first* clearly identifies which book, so *A Boy's Will* is parenthetical.)

8) no comma before or after *A Boy's Will* (Frost wrote several books of poems. *A Boy's Will* tells which of Frost's book is meant, so it's not parenthetical.)

Chapter 7—

Figures of Speech: Numerical Terms in English

When arithmetic meets language, people are often at sixes and sevens. They don't know whether to eighty-six old terms like *semi-annual* or *biannual* or call the five-oh about *four-flushers*. They're divided over the use of *fraction*. They want the 411 on *majority* vs. *plurality* and the whole nine yards on the correct use of *decimate*.

Let's put a little English on the eight ball and zero in on a number of number terms.

Majority rules

Sorry, wrong number!

That's what I said when I read these sentences:

"The tornado decimated 80 percent of the trailer homes."

"Only a fraction of Americans are millionaires."

"In the election of 1860, Lincoln received a majority of the popular votes."

"The proliferation of nuclear weapons is a great dilemma of our time."

I demand a recount! Here's why:

- **decimate**—The original meaning of *decimate* was to kill every tenth soldier, often as a way of enforcing discipline in the ranks (which explains why brutal generals often boasted about being able to "count on" their men.) Since then, *decimate* has also come to mean to destroy a large part of a group, a usage now accepted by nine out of ten linguists.

But less "ten"able in these experts' eyes is the use of *decimate* to mean to destroy a single object completely ("The fire decimated the house"). What's even worse, they say, is using *decimate* with any specific number other than ten percent, as in, "The tornado decimated 80 percent of the trailer homes."

- **fraction**—Some people object to this use of *fraction* to mean a small portion. They claim *fraction* can mean any percentage of something, even big percentages, e.g. five sixths, seven eighths, etc.

  The anti-*fraction* faction contends your logic is seriously fractured if you say *fraction* when you mean tiny percentage. Their opponents reply that this minor infraction is no cause for infarction. While technically *fraction* can refer to any percentage, they say it's now generally accepted to mean a small percentage.

- **majority**—*Majority* means winning more than 50 percent of all votes cast. *Plurality* means winning more votes than anyone else does. In the four-way presidential race of 1860, Lincoln garnered only a plurality of the popular vote (39 percent). But he won a majority of electoral college votes (180 of 303), en-Abe-ling him to be elected.

- **dilemma**—This word comes from the Greek words *di* (two) and *lemma* (propositions). Well into the 20th century, *dilemma* meant specifically a difficult choice between two unfavorable options. Because animals usually have two horns, we speak of "the horns of a dilemma," and that's no bull.

  But over the last 50 years a new meaning has horned in. *Dilemma* is now being used to refer to any general problem or predicament, even if it doesn't involve two options, e.g., "the dilemma of homelessness" or "the dilemma of nuclear proliferation."

Now I face a true dilemma: 1) I can tell you the use of *dilemma* to mean any predicament is now accepted by most experts (true), or 2) I can tell you some experts still object strongly to this general use (also true).

I choose 2. As someone once told the heroine of a Jane Austen novel, "Not every pickle is a true dil, Emma."

Gazillions of Googols

If big numbers sometimes do a number on you, I've got your number:

- **gazillions**—Let's start the bidding at a *thousand*, which is often abbreviated as *K* (short for *kilo*). Wholier than a *thou* is a *million* (a thousand thousand), and a *billion* (a thousand million).

Until recently, in parts of Europe, *billion* meant a million million (our trillion), but now all Europeans are thoroughly modern "Millies," using *billion* the same way our government does. Eeeek!

Beyond *trillion*, the "higher-archy" is supposed to run *quadrillion*, *quintillion*, (this is starting to add up!), *sextillion*, *septillion* etc., but, for such immense numbers, most of us prefer creative prefixes like *jillion*, *zillion*, *skillion* or *whomptillion*.

Another big number is *googol*. A *googol* is ten to the 100th power. The term *googol* was coined when mathematician Edward Kasner asked his 9-year-old nephew Milton to name the biggest number he could think of. Milton replied, "a googol!"

Milton, I'm glad your number came up. And if your number has already come up, I say, "Milton! Thou shouldst be living at this hour."

But the grand daddy of gigantic numbers is the *googolplex*—a googol to the googol power.

While a googol is 1 with 100 zeros following it, a *googolplex* is 1 followed by 10,000,000,000,000,000,000,000,000,000,000,000,

000,000,000,000,000,000,000,000,000,000,000,000,000,000,000,
000,000,000,000,000,000 zeros. That's ten million billion trillion
trillion, trillion, trillion, trillion, trillion, trillion zeros.

As Kasner put it, "There would not be enough room to write it, if
you went to the farthest star, touring all the nebulae and putting
down zeros every inch of the way."

Not to put down zeros or anything, but enough is enough!

- **legion**—In the Roman army, a legion consisted of anywhere from
  MMM to MMMMMM soldiers, based on the appreciative sounds
  made by Roman maidens when 3,000-6,000 Fabio look-alikes
  marched by.

  Today *legion* (from the Old French) is not foreign to us. It means
  any large number and can even be used as an adjective, as in "Fabio's
  admirers are legion."

- **host**—The enemies (*hostes*) of the Roman legions were usually
  numerous, so, in English, *host* means army or multitude. (Even if
  you invite a host of enemies to your home, *host*, meaning to enter-
  tain, comes from a different Latin word, *hospes*, meaning a guest.)

- **myriad**—In ancient Greece, *myriad* meant a very specific number—10,000. (When *The Iliad* sold 10,000 copies, for instance,
  some called it *The Myriad.*) Over the centuries, however, *myriad*
  became a roamin' numeral, signifying a very large but very indefi-
  nite number.

  But is *myriad* an adjective or a noun? Yes. Although *myriad* was
  originally used only as a noun in English, the adjective *myriad*
  was well entrenched by the end of World War I, to say nothing of
  myriad soldiers.

  Now a myriad of people use *myriad* in myriad ways, and it can
  even modify a singular noun to mean diverse ("the myriad tragedy
  of war").

Given *myriad*'s myriad life, will the rock group 10,000 Maniacs soon change its name to "Myriad Maniacs"? Will Minnesota's license plate soon read, "Land of Myriad Lakes"?

I wouldn't count on it.

A lesson in less

Should the sign over the express lane in the supermarket read, "Ten items or less," or "Ten items or fewer"?

Good question. In fact, the debate over *fewer* and *less* has been raging in English for no (less? fewer?) than a thousand years. Step into the express lane for a second, and I'll give you the "Quik Chek" answer to your question:

"Ten items or fewer" is correct because *fewer* is usually used with separate, countable items ("fewer apples"). *Less* should always be used for a quantity that is thought of as a single unit ("less fruit").

Unfortunately, "ten items or less" is a sign of the times. More and more people are using *less* when they should use *fewer*, saying "less people," "less taxes" and "less regulations."

But let's step into the regular check-out lane and check out some instances when it's OK to use *less* with countable quantities.

Less is preferred when following the word *one* ("one less error") or when it appears in the idiom "no less than" ("no less than 30 people were there"). "Less than" is usually used with measures of distance, amount or time when these measures are thought of as amounts rather than numbers, as in "less than 400 miles," "less than $4,000," and "less than four weeks."

In such cases, trust your ear. After all, would you buy a used car from someone who said, "This car, which has fewer than 400 miles on it, is fewer than four weeks old and costs fewer than $4,000"?

Finally, "or less" is considered an acceptable idiom in "25 words or less." But, if "25 words or less" is valid," some experts argue, why do we condemn the same use in "ten items or less"?

In 25 words or less, here's why: That's the zany nature of idioms. *Less* is OK in the idiom "words or less," but not OK in the non-idiomatic "items or less."

Over and out

Is it wrong to say "over a thousand dollars" when you mean "more than a thousand dollars"?

That's a grand question.

Over has been used for centuries to mean more than. My favorite citation of this use comes from Henry Thoreau who, finding himself saddled with unsold copies of his first book, wrote wryly, "I have now a library of nearly 900 volumes, over 700 of which I wrote myself."

In fact, it was another 19th-century American author, William Cullen Bryant, who first engaged in *over* kill. In 1877, as editor of the *New York Evening Post*, Bryant, for unexplained reasons, forbade his reporters to use *over* to mean more than. (The headline in the *Post* the next day read, "Bryant to *Over*: Drop Dead!").

Over the last century, newspaper editors and stylebooks have bent *over* backwards, trying to explain why *over* shouldn't replace *more than*—without much success. The Associated Press, for instance, resorts to a Jimminy Cricket approach, admitting in its stylebook that *over* can be used with numerals, but cautioning, "Let your ear be your guide."

For my guide, I'll use Kyff's First Law of Term-odynamics: Choose the least ambiguous word. (Here's where I put on my white lab coat.)

Over is sometimes ambiguous because it has so many meanings: more than, above, again, during, etc. For instance, the sentence, "Officials in helicopters counted over 100,000 people," could mean either that officials counted more than 100,000 people, or that they counted 100,000 people for a second time, or that they counted while flying above the people.

Similarly, "He lived in the subway over 20 years," could mean he lived there more than 20 years or for 20 years.

By the same token, however, *more than* is less than perfect when it comes to ambiguity. For instance, the sentence, "Jane owns more than 40 apartments," could mean she owns in excess of 40 apartments or that she owns many other things besides 40 apartments, such as a car, a house and a boat.

Even so, *more than* is generally less ambiguous than *over*. Based on the First Law of Term-odynamics, "more than" wins me over.

Phrases you can count on

- **third degree**—This term has nothing to do with degree in the legal ("third degree murder") or medical sense ("third degree burns"). It's derived from the secret fraternal organization called the Freemasons, and refers to the rigorous tests given to those seeking to become third-degree Masons. Even though the Masons' examinations generally didn't involve physical or mental coercion, *third degree* came to describe the use of brutality or torture to elicit information from a prisoner.

- **fourth estate**—By tradition, the three estates in Britain are kings, lords and commons, while in some other nations they're the nobility, clergy and middle class. Novelist Henry Fielding used the term *fourth estate* in 1750 to describe the mob, but its first use to refer to journalists occurred in 1826 when Thomas Macaulay wrote, "The gallery in which the reporters sit has become a fourth estate of the realm." Macaulay was recognizing the fact that journalists had become a powerful force in British politics—a "real estate," if you'll pardon the expression.

- **fifth column**—In 1836, during the Spanish Civil War, rebel general Queipo de Llano radioed to Loyalist forces in Madrid, "We have four columns on the battlefield against you and a fifth column inside your ranks." Ever since then, *fifth column* has referred to a secret subversive organization working within a country to assist an invading enemy.

- **at sixes and sevens**—To be *at sixes and sevens* means to be in a state of confusion. Parents who have hosted a birthday party for 6- and 7-year olds might think they've pinned the tail on this term's etymological donkey, but its origins are dicier.

  Some say it comes from medieval dice games in which rolling a six or a seven had special significance. Geoffrey Chaucer, known for putting a little Olde English on his dice throws, used "set on six and seven" to mean risk one's fortune. Presumably, someone who was always gambling, i.e., betting on sixes and sevens, would find his finances in disarray.

  Other experts say *sixes and sevens* comes from point-counterpoint arguments favored by small children and small-minded adults ("Is so!"—"Is not!"). While debating the number of Snow White's dwarfs, for instance, one kid might yell, "Six!" and the other, "Seven!" thus remaining at sixes and sevens until one gets Grumpy.

- **twenty-three skiddoo!**—Everyone agrees that *skiddoo* in this catch phrase of the early 1900s comes from *skedaddle*, a word of unknown origin meaning to leave hastily, flee. *Skiddoo* was popularized by cartoonist T. A. "Tad" Dorgan at the turn of the century. (At first I wondered where Dorgan got the nickname "Tad"—but only initially.)

  Linguist John Ciardi says *23 skiddoo!* began as a variant of the race starter's command "1-2-3-go!," which became "1-2-3-skiddoo!" Soon the rushed syllables "2-3" were being rendered as "23" to produce *23 skiddoo!*

Meanwhile, author Bill Bryson has traced the term to the Flatiron Building in New York City. Supposedly this skyscraper's triangular shape created unusual drafts that lifted the skirts of female pedestrians passing on 23rd Street. Soon groups of men began hanging out on 23rd Street, hoping for a favorable breeze. The police periodically dispersed these voyeurs with the command, "Hey, you—23 skiddoo!"

Unfortunately, this uplifting explanation probably skirts the truth.

- **eighty-six**—This means to kill or get rid of something. When restaurant servers, for instance, tell a cook to eighty-six the corn, they mean to can it. Some blokes say *eighty-six* is an Americanization of a Cockney slang term rhyming with *nix*.

  Others eighty-six this notion, saying it originated at the Greenwich Village restaurant Chumley's, which has a rear door at 86 Bedford Street. During Chumley's more boisterous days as a speakeasy, disorderly chums were sometimes tossed out through the back door, and thus eighty-sixed.

The whole nine yards

Ever since Zeus first birdied the ninth hole with a 9-iron on Mount Olympus, the number 9 has enjoyed mystical status in Western culture. (According to myth, one of Zeus' divots landed in the Mediterranean and became Crete—an unexpected "divot end" for the Greek tourist industry.)

Given this holy pedigree, *nine* is often associated with the best or most of anything, as the following *nine*-isms suggest:

- **dressed to the nines**—Some visionaries see this term, which means all dressed up, as a derivation of the Middle English "to then eynes" (eyes). Others say *nines* came to represent the summit of perfection because the number 9 (a trio of holy trinities) once stood for religious perfection.

Musing on this subject, I prefer a third explanation: *Nines* refers to the nine Muses, who in Greek and Roman mythology presided over artistic pursuits such as poetry and music. Thus, anyone whose artistry approached the excellence of these paragons was compared to the Nines, the way we might compare outstanding vocalists to "The Supremes."

- **on cloud nine**—Some say this expression, meaning a state of bliss, is a reference to the highest of the nine celestial spheres postulated by ancient astronomers. Others credit it to meteorology's International Classification of Clouds, which designates one of the highest cloud types, cumulonimbus, as *cloud nine*.

  Instead, I like John Ciardi's equally airy explanation: On a 1950s radio show, comedian Johnny Dollar would pretend to be knocked out and then wake up blabbering about the happiness he had just experienced on "cloud nine." Soon Dollar's coinage gained currency.

- **the whole nine yards**—There are two different explanations for this idiom for the entirety of something, and neither has anything to do with yards of fabrics or football fields. Some say it originated with old-style concrete trucks on which a full load of concrete comprises nine cubic yards. So a customer who wanted a full truckload of concrete would ask for "the whole nine yards."

  But others machine-gun that explanation, tracing the term to the ammunition belts of guns on World War II fighter planes, which were exactly nine yards long. So a pilot who had used all his ammo in a fight was said to have given the enemy "the whole nine yards."

Here's the 411 on number slang

Here's the 411 (information) on some jive that counts:

If you witness someone *eighty-sixed* (murdered) with a *four pounder* (handgun, from its weight), call the *5-0* (police) to report a *187* (murder).

The term *5–0* surfed in from the TV series *Hawaii 5–0*, while *187* is the numerical designation for murder in the California penal code.

The 5–0 are on duty *24/7* (24 hours a day, seven days a week—in other words, all the time). And speaking of surfing, *hang ten* (toes off the surfboard) means take a risk, do it to the max.

The 5–0 also handle mundane crimes like *five-finger discounts*, a term for shoplifting that first jumped off the shelf in the 1930s. Other digital expressions you should keep handy include *high five*, *give me five* and *five on five* (a handshake).

Someone taking a five-finger discount might steal a *forty* or a *sixty-four* (a 40-ounce or 64-ounce bottle of beer, respectively), or an *eight ball* (a bottle of Olde English 800 malt liquor.) Before being caught, a shoplifter tries to *5000* (leave), from Audi 5000, as in, "I'm 'audi' (outta) here."

Flappers of the 1920s referred to a tough customer as an *eight minute* (a guy as hard as an egg boiled for eight minutes). Flappers also did a number on *forty-niners* (men prospecting for a rich wife), *dime boxes* (taxi cabs, from their price) and *four-flushers* (poker players who pretend to have a five flush when they really only have four cards of the same suit).

The beats of the 1950s "totaled" us with *four bars past* (very), *Fifth Avenue* (good) and a *blast and a half* (a really good party). Add-ons of the 1960s include *do a number* (defeat or abuse), *seven-ply gasser* (seven times sensational), *288* (too gross, literally two times 144, a gross), and *throw a seven* (to have bad luck or lose one's poise, from craps, where a player loses when a seven is rolled).

The 1980s and 1990s have given us *six-pack* (what the six abdominal muscles on a well-built torso look like), *take it down a thousand* (calm down), and *L-7* (a square, from the shape made by forming an L and a 7 with your fingers (*L7*)

Monster Mash

Can you spot the monstrous grammar and usage errors in this conversation between Dr. Frankenstein and his assistants Igor and Lee? (Look for the hidden clue in the wording of each sentence.)

1) **Dr. Frankenstein:** I'm anxious to sew this monster together, Igor, so please give me a hand.

2) **Igor:** My, my, Master. I didn't realize that you objected to me taking a break.

3) **Lee:** Working on this monster, it appears that one of his parts is dangling.

4) **Dr. Frankenstein:** Only sew those parts that are loose, and place them as carefully as you would your own, Lee.

5) **Lee:** While I'm sewing, can I ask you a question about creating an extra monster next May.

6) **Dr. Frankenstein:** Lee, you seem to like this work better than him. He, he!

Answers:

1) If Dr. Frankenstein were eager to please language purists, he would say, "I'm eager (not *anxious*) to sew this monster together, Igor."

2) "My, my," say the experts, declaring that Igor should say "my taking a break," not "me taking a break." That's because a gerund (*taking*) should be preceded by a possessive pronoun (*my*). (But if Igor were trying to emphasize that Dr. Frankenstein objected to HIM taking a break, *taking* becomes a participle and should be preceded by *me*.)

3) In fact, it's the participial phrase "working on this monster" that's dangling. It should be surgically reattached to the sentence by adding the subject *I*. ("Working on this monster, I noticed that one of his parts is dangling.")

4) Dr. Frankenstein did not place *only* carefully. "Only sew those parts that are loose" means that loose parts should only be sewn as opposed to being stapled or glued, for example). Clarify the meaning by placing *only* after *sew* as in, "sew only those parts that are loose."

5) Can. Use *may*. Lee surely can ask about creating an extra monster next May, but what he means is "May I ask about it?"

6) If Lee likes his work better than he likes Igor, it should be "than him." But if, as Dr. Frankenstein seems to suggest, Lee likes his work better than Igor does, it should be "than he" because "than he does" is implied.

Hee, hee!

Chapter 8—

Swing Shifts: How Words Change in Meaning

The highway of English is slippery—so slippery, in fact, that it's not unusual for a word to do a 180-degree turn in meaning. As Bill Bryson notes in his delightful book *The Mother Tongue, counterfeit* once meant a legitimate copy, *brave* connoted cowardice, and *egregious* once meant admirable.

The comment of King James II when he first saw St. Paul's Cathedral in the 1600s provides a flying buttress for this theory. He called this work of Christopher Wren (no relation to Christopher Robin) "awful, artificial and amusing." Based on today's meaning of these words, he was pooh-poohing it.

In fact, he loved it. Back then, *awful* meant deserving of awe, *amusing* meant amazing, and *artificial* meant full of skillful artifice. A triple 180!

From rags to riches and vice versa

Five hundred years ago, if you called your neighbor a "cunning villain," he might thank you for the compliment. But describe him with the same words today, and he'll never lend you his hedge clippers again. For in medieval times, *cunning* meant knowledgeable, not sly, and *villain* meant villager, not scoundrel.

These words, like many others that originally bore positive denotations in English, have acquired negative or disparaging meanings over the centuries. Like patricians turned paupers, they're now slumming it through the back alleys of English.

Linguists, who seem to have a word for everything, call this riches-to-rags depreciation of meaning *pejoration*, from the Latin root *peior* (worse). Words that have suffered pejoration include *puny*, which originally meant younger; *cretin*, which originally meant Christian; and *lewd*, which originally meant of the laity. *Obsequious* and *crafty* once meant flexible and skilled, respectively (and respectably).

But how does this happen?

Usually, a word's meaning changes subtly and gradually over many decades or centuries, and often the shift in meaning is logical and understandable. *Clown* and *boor*, for instance, both originally meant farmer, and it's easy to see how snobbish city-dwellers might associate these words with comedic or uncouth behavior, respectively. Likewise, *scavenger* meant tax collector; *naughty* meant worthy of notice; and *silly* meant holy, innocent.

The reasons for other shifts in meaning are more mysterious. How did *egregious*, for instance, which once meant admirable, come to mean offensive? How did *garble*, which once meant sort out, come to mean mix up? How, in African-American English, did *bad* come to mean good?

While English words do seem to have a penchant for assuming derogatory and "lower" meanings, many words have also climbed the social ladder, a process linguists call *melioration*. *Guy*, for instance, once meant a person of grotesque appearance or dress; *pioneer* meant a common foot soldier; *yen* meant craving for opium; *revolutionary* meant deeply subversive, radical; *lean* meant gaunt, emaciated; and *urbane* meant urban.

Naughty and nice

Perhaps the best example of changing meanings is *nice*, a word that wasn't always so nice. Its stock has gyrated in value wildly over the centuries.

Derived from the Latin *nescire* (to be ignorant), *nice* scraped along as a penny stock in the 14th century, bearing lowly meanings such as foolish, ignorant and stupid.

During the 15th century it upticked slightly to mean lascivious, loose. When, for instance, Shakespeare spooned out, "For when my hours were nice and lucky," he was referring to the wanton soup of youthful dissipation.

In the 16th century, *nice* rallied to mean extravagant, elegant, tender. But during the 17th century it slipped into over-refined, intricate, difficult, coy, as in "nice Morn," John Milton's description of a teasing sunrise.

In the 19th century, *nice* rose again to mean refined, cultured, discriminating. The last meaning survives in our phrase, "that's a nice distinction."

And *nice*, of course, has been the growth stock of the 20th century—a real blue chip. As our number-one word meaning agreeable, pleasant, this most recent *nice* guise finishes first.

Doing 360s on the highway of English

Perhaps the most fascinating semantic skids are the full 360s—words that spin around and come back full circle to their original meanings.

Collaborator, for instance, which took on negative connotations during World War II as a person working for the enemy, a traitor, is now returning to its original meaning as a partner in an intellectual endeavor.

Notorious, which originally meant widely known, soon came to mean disreputable, infamous. But now, much to the consternation of purists, people are increasingly using *notorious* in its original sense of famous with no derogatory implications.

According to my calculations, *calculus* is currently performing a classic 360. Back in the 1600s, *calculus* was often used as a general term for computation or calculation. In 1693, for instance, when astronomer Edmund Halley wrote about a "calculus founded on the experience of a very great number of years," he meant a calculation, rather than a branch of mathematics.

Eventually, this general calculation meaning of *calculus* died out. For a long time dictionaries listed only this word's narrow mathematical and scientific definitions: integral and differential calculus, an abnormal accretion in the body, and dental tartar. (And if you think I'm going to try to explain the difference between integral and differential calculus, you'd better recalculate.)

But now, like Halley's comet, the general meaning of *calculus* is returning to our semantic solar system. As these quotations show, journalists are particularly fond of it: "the obsession with Dole recalls Richard Nixon's political calculus"; "here's how the political calculus looks."

In English, as in life, what goes around, comes around. You can add the "360 factor" to your linguistic calculus.

Wherefore art thou, meaning?

One reason high school students often have so much trouble understanding William Shakespeare's works is that the original meanings of many words the bard used have since been disbarred.

The classic example is Juliet's query, "O Romeo! Romeo! Wherefore art thou Romeo?" In Shakespeare's time, *wherefore* meant, not where, but why, so Juliet is asking, not "Where are you?" but "Why do you have to be Romeo, a member of the hated Montague family?"

Likewise, when Romeo says, "Show me a mistress that is passing fair," he's not saying he's willing to settle for a woman whose beauty was merely passable. *Passing* was short for *surpassingly*; he wanted a knockout.

And, after Romeo and the passing fair Juliet have passed away, Benvolio tells the Prince, "I can discover all." Here he means, not that he'll find out what happened, but that he'll disclose or uncover all.

These Hamlet-like shifts in word meanings are particularly notable in, appropriately, *Hamlet*. In the very first scene of the play, for instance, the watchman Bernardo describes Horatio and Marcellus as the "rivals of my watch," which might make you think they were intruders or competitors for his job. But, in Shakespeare's time, *rival* meant a companion or associate in a particular duty.

Later in the play, when Polonius describes Hamlet's behavior as "the very ecstasy of love," *ecstasy* means madness, not joy. And when Hamlet complains of the world that "things rank and gross in nature possess it merely," *merely* doesn't mean in a small way, simply, but, instead, its opposite, completely. And you might wonder why Hamlet wants to wipe away "fond records" from his memory until you realize that *fond* meant, not cherished, but foolish.

More foul play occurs when Hamlet says, of his father's death, "I doubt some foul play." In fact, Hamlet thinks foul play has occurred. That's because Shakespeare's *doubt* meant, not to distrust or to disbelieve, but to suspect.

And when Hamlet vows to follow his father's ghost and to kill anyone "that lets me," *lets* doesn't mean allow but its opposite, hinder. This archaic sense of *let* to mean obstruct still survives among courtly pros—in tennis, where a ball that hits the net is called a "let ball."

Facile fossils

Did you ever wonder why *bravado* doesn't mean bravery, but instead a false show of courage?

In fact, *bravado* is a linguistic fossil. It retains a meaning that *brave* has since lost: pretending to be courageous. Like a dinosaur bone in a rock bed, *bravado* provides hard evidence that a not-so-brave *brave* once roamed the Earth.

Today we speak of "neck" of the woods," "kith and kin" and "bank teller," probably not realizing that *neck* once meant a piece of land, *kith* meant neighbors, and *tell* meant to count.

Likewise, we throw our *suitcases* and other *luggage* into the *trunks* of our cars. But, chances are, those suitcases don't contain suits, and we've forgotten that *luggage* is a fancy word for something we have to lug, and that cars once had actual trunks lashed to their rear bumpers.

As technology progresses, language sometimes lags. In fact, many commonly used terms are anachronistic fossils whose original associations are now almost forgotten.

We use seat belts and air bags to prevent our heads from dashing on the front instrument panel of our cars, for instance, without really thinking about the origin of the term *dashboard*. We forget that our *fenders* fend off other cars, and that our *tires* are so called because they attire the wheel. And when was the last time you used the *glove compartment* to hold gloves?

In fact, I need only look as far as the computer keyboard in front of me to see word ghosts dancing. The key that makes capital letters, for instance, is labeled *shift* because on typewriters the entire carriage shifted to make a capital letter.

Likewise, the *return* key, now used not only to move the cursor to the left margin, but to indicate "OK, do it!" is so labeled because the roller on a typewriter physically returned to its original position on the left to begin a new line.

On computers, we move through a multi-page document by *scrolling*, just as ancient scribes unrolled long scrolls. Standard page patterns are called *templates*, a word that goes back not only to thin metal plates used in woodworking and metal fabrication, but also to *temple*, a device on a loom that keeps the cloth stretched during weaving.

In cyberspace, Gates meets Gutenberg. When we create a page on a computer, for instance, we click on *paste* to fix text in place, just as old-fashioned printers used adhesive to paste in galleys. We click on *font* to select a typeface because the Old French *fondre* meant to melt, and the first typesetters melted down metal to make type. And we then type in *cutlines* (captions under photographs) because, when traditional printers make a negative of a page, the spaces where photos go are literally cut out.

But my favorite fossil of all is *c.c.* Even though we're several technological revolutions removed from carbon copies, we still use this abbreviation to indicate who's getting copies of a memo or letter. Talk about carbon dating!

And, speaking of carbon dating, let's monitor the thoughts of the re"noun"ed linguistic paleontologist U. Stew Mean as he examines other fossil words...

Hmmmm. Here's a mincemeat pie. Funny, unlike most mincemeat pies, there's no meat in it, but plenty of fruit.

Perhaps *meat* used to mean any kind of food or nourishment, not just the flesh of an animal. After all, the biblical phrase "meat and drink" means food and drink. That's it!

And here's a worm fence around a garden. It snakes around hillside farm fields like a serpent. Maybe *worm* used to mean any crawling animal, including snakes. That's it!

And here's the Forest of Bowland in Lancashire, England, where people love to hunt. Funny thing is, large parts of it are nearly treeless. Maybe *forest* once meant any big tract of land set aside for hunting, whether it had trees or not. After all, much of New Forest in Hampshire, England has no trees. That's it!

Look at that deer fly. It bites not only deer, but also a wide variety of animals, including horses and humans. Maybe *deer* once meant any kind of animal. After all, Shakespeare refers to "mice and rats, and such small deer." That's it!

And here's the deer fly that bit the worm that ate the meat that grew on the farm that stood in the forest that Jack deforested. Hmmmm.

Gender-benders

Did you know that *girl* once referred to a child of either gender? That *shrew* once denoted a male, and that *man* indicated a man or woman?

In fact, several of our most common English words have done some blatant gender bending over the centuries, usually following one of three patterns of cross dressing:

1) Positive terms that were once gender-neutral were turned into masculine words. The original meaning of *man*, for instance, was the unisex *human being*; only later did it assume the "man"tle of maleness. Likewise, *god*, now a masculine word, is derived from the Indo-European root *gheu-*, which denoted a deity of a neuter gender.

2) Independently formed words for females were misinterpreted as derivatives of *male* and *man*. *Female*, for instance, is not *male* with a *fe-* attached. (Such a male would be known as a gigolo.) Instead, *female* began as the independent Latin root *femina*, which in turn became the French *femelle*.

   But during the 14th century, when the French word *femelle* crossed the Channel, some linguistic channels also got crossed. The *melle* in *femelle* was mistakenly pronounced as *male*, so *femelle* became *female*. This egregious "male"-apropism led to the mistaken impression that *male* and *female* came from the same place, whereas we now know that women are from Venus and men are from Mars.

   Through similar "male"-feasance, the independent origin of *woman* was also erased. *Woman* came from the Old English *wifman*, with *wif* meaning *female* and *man* meaning a human being of either sex. Eventually, *wifman* became *wimman* and then *woman*, which was erroneously assumed to be an offspring of the male *man* (though some suspected the milkman).

3) Several diminutive or negative terms once applied to both genders came to denote females only. Like *man*, the word *girl* was

once gender neutral. But perhaps because children occupied a low status in medieval England, *girl* narrowed in definition to mean a female child around 1375 when a royal pronouncement chauvinistically decreed, "Boys will be boys!"

Similarly, *harlot*, a word now used for females only, originally meant a male vagabond or rascal, while a *wench* was a child of either sex, and a *shrew* was a male villain.

Far be it from me to suggest that English-speaking males deliberately appropriated gender neutral terms for themselves, turned independently coined words for women into male derivatives, and relegated negative words to females. But if the *shrew* fits, wear it.

Fifteen goin' on sixteen

Can you find 15 grammatical or usage errors in these sentences?

1) If I was you, I'd find out whose responsible.
2) Jane is equally as qualified as myself.
3) Neither they nor she believe it will have any affect on me getting promoted.
4) Chrysler has introduced their new model and it looks like its popular.
5) Wandering among the gardens, the flowers enchanted us for awhile.
6) The principle reason he was fired is because he's one of those people who doesn't cooperate with others.

Answers:

1) If I were you, I'd find out who's responsible. Use the subjunctive *were* to express conditions contrary to fact. You can't be another person, so it's *were*. *Who's* is a contraction of "who is." *Whose* is a possessive pronoun ("Find out whose coat this is"). And, no, it's not "whom is responsible;" the entire clause "who is responsible" functions as the direct object of "find out."

2) Jane is as qualified as I. *Equally* is redundant. Avoid using *myself* as a substitute for *I* or *me*; in this case, it's *I*, because you mean, "as I (am)."

3) Neither they nor she believes it will have any effect on my getting promoted. When subjects are joined by *either…or*, or *neither…nor*, the verb agrees with the subject closer to it. *Effect* means influence, consequence. The noun *affect* is used by psychologists to mean feeling, emotion. A possessive pronoun (*my*) should precede the gerund *getting*, unless you're emphasizing it's me who's getting promoted.

4) Chrysler has introduced its new model and it looks as if it's popular. Use the singular *its*, not *they*, to refer to the singular noun. *As if*, not *like*, should introduce a clause of comparison. Don't confuse the possessive *its* with *it's*, the contraction for "it is."

5) Wandering among the gardens, we were enchanted by the flowers for a while. The participial phrase "wandering among the gardens" describes *we*, not "the flowers." The adverb *awhile* never follows a preposition (*for*), but "we rested awhile" is fine.

6) The principal reason he was fired is that he's one of those people who don't cooperate with others. Don't confuse the noun *principle* (a rule or belief) with the noun and adjective *principal* (a key person, foremost). "Reason is…because" is redundant. After "one of those people who," use the plural verb *don't* because you're really saying, "of those people who don't cooperate with others, he is one."

Chapter 9—

Lost in Translation: Foreign Words in American English

When English imports words from foreign languages, strange things can happen. For instance, English speakers assumed the Old French word for a cherry, *cherise*, was a plural. So instead of referring to a cherry as a *cherise*, they dropped the *s* sound and called it a *cherry*. Words and phrases such as "that's the ticket" and "May Day!" resulted from similarly loose interpretations of French words.

Likewise, we often use Greek and Latin expressions freely with little or no understanding of their pronunciations or meanings. Is *antennae* pronounced *an-ten-ee* or *an-ten-eye*? Is there such a thing as a *kudo*?

But what perhaps creates the most confusion are the vast differences between the English of the United States and that of Great Britain—two nations, as George Bernard Shaw said, "separated by a common language." So, with a cheery, cherry cheerio, I say Tallyho!

False plurals cross Urals

"Pease porridge hot/pease porridge, cold/pease porridge in the pot/nine days old."

Did you ever wonder what the *pease* in this popular nursery rhyme referred to? Come to think of it, did you ever wonder what nine-day-old porridge would taste like?

Once upon a time, *pease* was the Middle English word for *pea*. Its plural was *peasen*. Then, one day, someone assumed that *pease*, because it ended in an *s* sound, was actually a plural of a word that didn't exist—*pea*. And so *pea* was planted. (This story is recounted in the fairy tale "The Prince's *S* and the Pea.")

Gradually, *pea* spread like kudzu through English, its plural became *peas*, and *pease* was purged from everything but that porridge.

Mistaking a singular foreign word ending with an *s* sound for a plural is quite common in English. For example, when a fortified wine with a nutty flavor made in Xeres, Spain, was introduced to England in the 1500s, the English called it *sherris*, their best approximation of *Xeres*. Assuming *sherris* to be a plural, they soon toasted the birth of a new English word—*sherry*.

The English landed in this same trap when they mistook the Scottish singular word *teaz* (a place where something is poised or held ready) for a plural, and teed up the word *tee*.

French words have been especially vulnerable to such misinterpretation. Mistaking the French singular *sucours* (help, aid) for a plural, the English coined *succor*.

Likewise, the English assumed the French word *richesse* (richness, wealth) was a plural, and made it so in their own language—*riches*, though, oddly, the singular noun form *rich* never appeared. They also horsed around with the French word *chaise* (a light, open carriage), dragging it into English as a plural, and harnessing it to a singular—*shay*.

And, if you think such linguistic horseplay only occurred in olden days, think again. The same thing happens right now in English whenever someone mistakes the Greek word *kudos* (praise) for a plural and awards someone a *kudo*.

Saying *kudo* is as absurd as treating the singular Greek nouns *bathos*, *pathos* and *hubris* as plurals and saying *batho*, *patho* and *hubri*. Such acts of hubris won't earn you kudos from usage purists.

The French had a word for it

Captain: May Day! May Day! We've hit a reef. Taking on water fast. Over.

Coast Guard: Roger. I've got you spotted on radar now. By the way, did you know the distress call *May Day* has nothing to do with the spring celebration on the first of May or the communist holiday observed the same day? It actually evolved when English speakers mispronounced the French word *m'aidez*, the last part of the phrase *venez m'aidez*, meaning come help me. Over.

Captain: I don't care if it came from Vinnie the maitre d'! Not everything is in apple-pie order here, if you catch my tilt, which is what this boat's beginning to do. Over.

Coast Guard: Wilco. Don't get crusty with me. "Apple pie order," by the way, comes not from a neatly baked pie, but from a mispronunciation of the French phrase "nape plié en ordre," meaning linens folded neatly. In England during the period following the Norman conquest, when a French lord ordered his Anglo-Saxon maid to keep the "nape plié en ordre," the maid, who spoke only English, probably heard his words as "apple pie order." Over.

Captain: Here's a real order: If we sink, send a forlorn hope. Over.

Coast Guard: Roger. Did you realize that the seeming oxymoron "forlorn hope," which means a desperate undertaking or an extremely hazardous mission, is actually an English misunderstanding of the Dutch phrase "verloren hoop," which means neither forlorn nor hope, but advance guard? Over.

Captain: *I'm* becoming forlorn and hopeless. Send help! I don't care whether it's a forlorn hope or Bob Hope. Over.

Coast Guard: A rescue vessel is on the way. Over.

Captain: That's the ticket. Over.

Coast Guard: You're not gonna' believe this, but "that's the ticket" is an English mispronunciation of the French word *etiquette*. The phrase "that's etiquette," meaning that's the correct thing, came to be rendered as "that's 'uh-tick'ut" and eventually, "that's the ticket."

Captain: No kidding. Out, or, as they say in French, "Oh Revolve!"

Boning up on bona fide

If you've ever thought *ad hoc* was a winter sport, *sui generis* was a Chinese dish or *magnum opus* was a handgun, here's your chance to bone up on the bona fide meanings of commonly used Latin idioms.

- **in medias res** (in-MAY-dee-ahs-RACE), literally "into the middle of things," means in the middle of a sequence of events or literary work. If, for instance, you entered a screening of the film *Pulp Fiction in media res*, you might be very confused about what's going on. Then again, if you had watched it from the beginning, you might be very confused about what's going on.

- **ad hominem** (ad-HAHM-uh-nem), literally "to the man," describes remarks that appeal to personal considerations rather than to issues. In political campaigns, for instance, some candidates ignore the issues and resort to *ad hominem* statements about their opponents. This never happens in the United States, of course.

- **ad hoc** (ad-HAHK), literally "for this," means something created for a specific purpose or situation immediately at hand, such as an *ad hoc* committee. Some dictionaries even accept the term "ad hocism" for the tendency to establish temporary policies, but most experts want to hock *ad hoc* used as a verb ("He wants to *ad hoc* health care reform").

- **de facto** (deh-FAK-toh), literally "from the fact," means in reality or actually. A *de facto* government rules a country in actuality, though lacking official authority, while a de faxo government rules solely by telecommunications.

- **sine qua non** (sin-i-kwah-NON), literally "without which not," is an essential element or condition. Turkey, for instance, is the *sin qua non* of a Thanksgiving feast. A reference to Julius Caesar is the *sine qua non* of any article on Latin.

Latin's ae *raises antennae*

In "Departmental," a poem about ants that's anti-New Deal, Robert Frost not only gives us a lesson about bureaucracy (lessen it), but a lesson in pronunciation as well. Describing one of the poem's ant-agonists, he rhymes,
"But he no doubt reports to any
With whom he crosses antennae"
If you pronounce *antennae* as "an-ten-eye", the rhyme doesn't work. But if you pronounce it correctly as "an-ten-ee," you're tuned in.

Figuring out how to pronounce the *ae* in Latin and Greek words adopted by English makes people antsy. Ironically, those who have studied Latin are probably most likely to mispronounce *ae* in English because *eye* is the correct pronunciation of these letters in Latin.

I can still remember exactly how my exacting Latin teacher Mr. Bodanza drilled us on the declension of the noun *agricola* (farmer): "agricola, agricolae" (a-grik-o-lye)…we repeated. This was enough to make us anti-farmer (or at least ant farmers), but I learned my lesson well. So it's no wonder that I want to say, "Aye, aye, Sir" whenever I see *ae* in a Latin word (or whenever I see anyone even slightly resembling Mr. Bodanza).

When spoken in English, however, Latin and Greek words containing *ae* are usually given a long *e* sound, as in *bee* (which, incidentally, is the grade I got in Mr. Bodanza's course). Thus, *aegis* (protection or sponsorship) is "ee-jis"; *alumnae* (female graduates) is "uh-lum-nee;" *vertebrae* (back bones) is "vur-tuh-bree"; and *Aesop* (author of that great fable about the ant and the grasshopper) is "ee-sup." I hate to harp on this, but even *Aeolian* is pronounced "e-o-le-an."

But beware: *ae* is not always pronounced "ee" in English. In *aerie* (high nest), *aerobic* (related to oxygen) and *aerosol* (a gaseous suspension), *ae* is pronounced with the "ay" sound of *air*. In *Aeschylus* and *aesthete*, it's pronounced like the *e* sound in *bet*. That's because the *ae* in these words comes from the Greek *aer* or *ais*, not from the Greek or Latin ligature Æ.

"Ligature?" That's the word for that funny construction where two letters run into each other like this, Æ, or like this, Œ. And when two ants run into each other, they cross antennae like this XX.

The English patient

A young man attacked a football coach with a catapult, a torch and a silencer.

If this scenario, replete with both modern and archaic weapons, were to be reported in an American newspaper, it would be a sinister, bizarre assault. But, if it appeared in the British press, it would be an account of banal, if eccentric vandalism: a young man attacked a soccer bus with a slingshot, flashlight and car muffler.

Whoever said that England and America are two countries separated by a common language was no *berk* (Britspeak for dweeb). (I wish I could remember who said that. Oh, pshaw!…That's it!—George Bernard Shaw. Or, as the Brits would say, George "BER-n'd" Shaw.)

Your Shaw-vinistic notions may be confirmed as you try to translate these British sentences into American:

1) The leading article next to the advert said the minister's plan to regulate corn prices should be tabled. (The editorial next to the advertisement said the cabinet member's plan to regulate wheat prices should be considered.)

2) He ordered bangers and porridge for breakfast, chips, prawns and crisps for lunch, along with his favorite sweets: jelly, biscuits and choc ice. (He ordered sausages and oatmeal for breakfast, french

fried potatoes, shrimp and potato chips for lunch, along with his favorite desserts: gelatin dessert, cookies and chocolate ice cream.)

3) While motoring anticlockwise on the orbital near the round about, he pulled his estate car onto the verge, lifted the bonnet, kicked the wing, opened the boot and pulled out a spanner. (While driving counterclockwise on the beltway near the traffic circle, he pulled his station wagon onto the shoulder, lifted the hood, kicked the fender, opened the trunk and pulled out a wrench.)

4) As the woman put on her smalls, dressing gown and plimsolls in the loo, her husband donned his vest, waistcoat, dinner jacket and braces. (As the woman put on her underwear, bathrobe and sneakers in the bathroom, her husband donned his undershirt, vest, tuxedo and suspenders.)

Sorry, old chaps. I have to chivvy (hurry along). Here are my last "inverted commas" (quotation marks) and final "full stop" (period).

Lost British words still thrive in colonies

If you told some British friends, "the ragamuffin in homespun whittles deftly," they would probably have no idea what you meant. Yet it's likely that their ancestors of 400 years ago would have understood every word.

Why? Because, during the 17th century, *ragamuffin, homespun, whittle* and *deft* were common words both in England and its American colonies. But while these terms still flourish in the United States, they've since died out in England.

During the 1600s, for instance, the English referred to autumn as the *fall*, just as we do now. But at some point, *fall* took its leave of England. Likewise, *gotten*, once widely used in Britain as the past participle of *get*, has gotten little use there for decades. Now Brits use *got* instead, as in, "We English have never quite got over losing the colonies, old chap." Quite.

Shakespeare's works, which were written at the time England was first colonizing America, include many words that took root in the New World but withered in the Old.

When Shakespeare wrote, for instance, in *Henry V, the Sequel,* "He is very sick, and would to bed" [sic], he was using *sick* in the general American sense of ill. In Britain today, *sick* specifically means nauseated. And in *Henry VI, the Final Judgment,* the bard used "I guess" to mean I suppose, a meaning that soon disappeared in Britain.

Several other words jumped into the American lifeboat just in time: *flapjack, platter, trash* (for rubbish), *skillet, mayhem, ornate, loan* (as in lend), *bureau, mad* (for angry), *professor, mean* (for cruel), *catty-corner, burly, magnetic, scant, loophole, chore, clodhopper* and *wilt.*

And, of course, many terms, once as dead as Marley in England, eventually returned to haunt Britain again as imports from America, including *maybe, quit* (in the sense of resign), *jeans* and *frame-up.* Ironically, some British Scrooges now condemn as "hum-bug Americanisms" the same terms their own ancestors once gleefully embraced.

Memo to Brits: We're glad to *loan* you your old words back, but this time don't let them *wilt.*

Some Scottish terms are out of kilter

It's time to scotch some common misuses of Scottish terms.

(The verb *scotch,* by the way, meaning to block or destroy, has nothing to do with Scotland. It comes from the Anglo-Norman *escocher,* meaning to cut, scratch or notch. The same root gives us *hopscotch,* a game in which children jump around lines they've scratched on the ground.)

Speaking of hopscotch, it's a bonny idea to hop over the word *Scotch* when referring to people from Scotland. Because the condescending British once used *Scotch* as a contraction of *Scottish,* many Scots regard the term as an insult.

This is actually a wee bit hypocritical because, 200 years ago, many people in Scotland referred to themselves as being *Scotch*. In fact, the Scots who departed for northern Ireland and America in the 1700s used the word freely, which is why *Scotch* has always been more acceptable in the U.S. than in Scotland.

Even so, it's wise to *Scotch* guard your sentences. Use *Scot* and *Scottish* to refer to people, and save *Scotch* for inanimate objects like Scotch broth, Scotch eggs and Scotch whiskey.

Did someone say *whiskey*? What we call *Scotch whiskey* in the U.S. is called simply *whisky* in Scotland. Some purists insist that all spirits distilled in Great Britain and Canada be spelled *whisky*, as opposed to the American *whiskey*, but most authorities ignore the dictate of these *whiskey* sours.

Finally, our use of *plaid* is out of kilter. In Scotland, *plaid* (pronounced "plade") is the shawl-like garment that Highlanders wear draped over their shoulders. The distinctive pattern woven into the fabric of a plaid, kilt or other garment is called a *tartan*.

Americans and the English, however, often use *plaid* to refer to the tartan (pattern) rather than to the shawl-like garment on which the tartan appears.

It's an easy and understandable mistake. Clothing makers do the same thing when they name colors or patterns after garments; a mail-order catalog, for instance, recently listed *fatigue* as a color choice (from army fatigues).

Nevertheless, true Scots insist that the use of *plaid* for *tartan* should be "kilt."

Get ready, et cet., go!

Can you spot seven errors involving Latin abbreviations in these seven sentences?:

1) Servius Tullius built fortifications on the seven hills of Rome, e.g., the Palatinus, the Capitolinus, the Quirinalis, etc.

2) He was one of seven Greek heroes (Adrastus, Polynices, etc.) who attacked Thebes.

3) The seven virtues are justice, temperance, charity and etc.

4) Pronouncing *etc.* as "et-set-ruh" is one of the seven deadly sins; it should be pronounced "et-set-uhr-uh."

5) The Seven Dwarfs, i.e., Doc, Bashful, Sleepy, Sneezy, Grumpy, Happy and, er…Fred, whistled while they worked. (I'm so dopey that I can't remember them all.)

6) The seven seas (Arctic, Antarctic et. al.) were celebrated in a Rudyard Kipling poem.

7) A week comprises seven days, viz., Sunday, Monday, Tuesday.

Answers:

1) Never use *etc.* following *e.g.* The abbreviation *e.g.*, short for the Latin "exempli gratia," means for example. Its use implies you're providing only a few examples, never all of the items. Because *etc.* suggests the inclusion of all items, it's illogical to use *etc.* following *e.g.*

2) Because *etc.* is an abbreviation for *et cetera*, which means "other things of the same kind," avoid using it with people. For people, use *et al.*, which is short for "and other things" or "and other people."

3) Because *et cetera* means "and other things," it's redundant to precede it with *and*.

4) Actually, *etc.* may be pronounced as three syllables ("et-set-ruh") or as four syllables ("et-set-uhr-uh"). Just don't say "ek-set-ruh" or "ek-set-uhr-uh."

5) The abbreviation *i.e.* stands for the Latin phrase "id est" (that is). It's almost always followed, not by a list or examples, but by a definition clarifying what preceded it, as in "The Seven Dwarfs, i.e. those little fellows who lived with Snow White." For lists (but not complete lists), use *e.g.*

6) Because *et* is the Latin word for *and*, not an abbreviation, it needs no period.

7) *Viz.*, short for the Latin *videlicet* ("it is permitted to see"), means namely. It's used when you want to itemize *all* the components of a collective noun, so in the quiz sentence it should be followed by all seven days of the week. (By the way, when spoken, *viz.* Is rendered as "namely."

Chapter 10—

Not To Worry:
Eight 'Rules' You Can Break

In the "never-never" land of our childhood, our parents and teachers warned us never to do certain things: Never play with matches, never run with lollipops in our mouths and never split infinitives.

Wisely following the first two rules, we've made it safely to adulthood, and some of us even have jobs. So we're probably old enough to finally learn the truth about the third rule: Sometimes it's OK to split an infinitive (as long as we don't have lollipops in our mouths at the time).

The prohibition on split infinitives is one of several old rules we can now sometimes ignore. Let's take a look at these nostrums to find out why they were formulated in the first place, and when it's safe to disregard them.

Never split an infinitive

An infinitive, you'll recall, is the basic form of a verb that includes the word *to*, as well as the verb itself. *To be*, *to do* and *to split* are all infinitives.

Because the infinitive forms of verbs in Latin are expressed as single words and thus cannot be split apart, Latin-loving 18th- and 19th-century grammarians somehow got the bright idea that English infinitives should be inviolate too and that an adverb should never come between *to* and its verb.

There's one teensy-weensy flaw with this rule: It makes no sense.

For instance, when I wrote in the introduction to this chapter that it was time for us "to finally learn" the truth, I could have avoided splitting the infinitive *to learn* by writing "finally to learn the truth" or "to learn finally the truth." But, if truth be told, my version is the smoothest and most natural of those three constructions.

The silly prohibition on split infinitives has obscured a more important rule: Always position your adverb to convey your meaning precisely. For instance, I could have split the infinitive in the preceding sentence and written, "to precisely convey your meaning," but since I wanted to emphasize the word *precisely*, I placed it at the end of the sentence.

Generally you should refrain from splitting an infinitive when doing so causes confusion or awkward rhythm. For instance, instead of writing, "It is sometimes wrong to completely, absolutely and totally separate a verb from *to*," you should write, "It is sometimes wrong to separate a verb completely, absolutely and totally from *to*."

Because hidebound traditionalists still regard splitting an infinitive as an occasion for side-splitting laughter, it's often better to follow dutifully (no split) silly regulations just to prove absolutely (no split) your mastery of rules it's OK to occasionally break (split).

Never end a sentence with a preposition

Because this rule is based on sound grammatical reasoning, it's nothing to sneeze at. But blindly following it in all cases is definitely something to guard against.

In most cases, ending a sentence with a preposition is like placing a nondescript boxcar at the end of a train instead of a bright red caboose. It's often a tip-off that the entire sentence has been assembled haphazardly.

Good writers of English, like good composers and boxers, want the final portions of each sentence, passage or flurry to end with punch. Thus we try to close the sentence with words that are important and decisive, or at least crisp and snappy.

Because a preposition merely expresses the relative position of two other words in a sentence, it's not often a great word to end a sentence with. Notice, for instance, how the preceding sentence seems to sputter out, and the final *with* sounds like the last gasp of a deflating balloon?

Some people try to repair such sentences by inserting an awkward *which* construction, as in, "It's not a great word with which to end a sentence." But, as you can see, using *which* can be clumsy and stiff.

Winston Churchill, for one, hated this kind of belabored formality. When an editor contorted one of Churchill's sentences to avoid a sentence-ending preposition, the Prime Minister replied: "This is the sort of arrant pedantry up with which I will not put!"

When you find yourself ending a sentence with a preposition, instead of resorting to *which* craft, completely rework the sentence. Thus, my sputtering balloon—"it's not often a great word to end a sentence with"—would be better written, "Ending a sentence with a preposition is not a great idea."

But some verbs followed by prepositions have become so commonly used as idioms that they sound perfectly natural at the end of a sentence. "His arrogance did him in," "I didn't know what was going on," and "She's someone you can work with" don't jar our ears.

And, in some sentences, we actually *do* want to emphasize the final preposition, as in, "He doesn't know what a turn signal is for," or "She didn't realize what this was all about."

For instance, the first two sentences in this section end with prepositions, but I'll bet they sounded all right to you.

Never say, 'It's me'; say, 'It's I'

A transcript of my recent telephone call to Buckingham Palace may help to explode this myth:

Word Guy: Is this the Queen?

Queen: This is she.

Word Guy: "This is *she*? Well, excuuuuse me! I hate to criticize Your Majesty, but aren't you getting a little bit highfalutin with this "she" stuff? Why not just plain "This is her"?

Queen: As a long, ancestral line of grammarians will tell you, a linking verb such as *am*, *is* or *are* must be followed by a predicate nominative, such as *I*, *he* or *she*, not a direct object such as *me*, *him* or *her*. It's decidedly ungrammatical to say, "This is her, or him, or me."

Word Guy: But it sounds so much more natural to say, "This is me," or, "It's her," or "It's them." Would you really jump out from behind a palace door and shout, "It's I!" or announce the arrival of a carload of guests by yelling, "It's they!"?

Queen: I generally don't lurk behind doors.

Word Guy: I suppose not. Look. It seems odd to be telling the Queen of the English-speaking world this, but, in English, there are action verbs and linking verbs. Action verbs are almost always followed by the objective case. We say, for instance, "This helps her," or "It pleases him," or "This surprises them."

Because we've heard objective case pronouns following action verbs so often, it seems natural to use them after linking verbs too, especially linking verbs we use a lot, such as the verb *to be*. So we say, "This is her," "It's him," and "This seems to be them." By contrast, saying, "This is she," "It's he," and "This seems to be they" sounds pompous and stuffy.

Queen: I beg your pardon.

Word Guy: No offense, but sometimes the vernacular language of your loyal subjects overrides imperial dictates. The commoners, through their everyday usage, are saying to the traditional grammarians, "You have met the enemy and it is us." There isn't much anyone can do about this, even if you prefer their saying, "You have met the enemy and it is we."

Queen: We are not amused.

Never begin a sentence with **And** *or* **But**

Sentences that start with *And* or *But* give many people starts. But I refuse to give such sentences a swift kick in the *But*.

Why? For starters, I'll quote you chapter and verse: "And God said, 'Let there be light'; and there was light. And God saw that the light was good." And who can argue with that?

The prohibition against starting a sentence with *And* probably had its genesis in The Book of Genesis when Adam and Eve tried to stop their son Cain from uttering sentences like, "Abel called me a serpent. And then he stole my fig leaf. And then he hit me."

And we all know where that spat ended!

As Cain's Raggedy *And* sentences demonstrate, it's rarely a good idea to begin several successive sentences with *And*. Repetitive *Ands* can give prose a droning, dreary tone. Likewise, starting too many sentences with *But* makes your writing choppy and abrupt.

These days we're most likely to encounter overuse of the sentence-starting *And* and *But* in newspaper editorials, which often swing back and forth between *And* and *But* like the pendulum of a clock: "And the President earns high marks…But he needs to address…And that will accomplish…But only time will tell."

But, when *And* is planted judiciously at the beginning of a sentence, it allows one sentence to flow smoothly from the previous one. And an opening *But* can provide desired shock value.

Advertising copywriters know this well. A Saab ad, for instance, includes sentences that begin, "And you might be surprised…" and "But then gas prices soared."

If citing a car ad as a paragon of usage makes you sob, would you trust the words of Thomas Jefferson? The Sage of Syntax could turn a king on his heel with a well-paced *But*. "Prudence, indeed, will dictate," he wrote in the Declaration of Independence, "that governments long established should not be changed for light and transient causes...*But* when a long train of abuses and usurpations..."

That was the *But* heard round the world.

Never use the possessive with an inanimate object

As schoolchildren, many of us were taught that it's wrong to use a possessive apostrophe with an inanimate object. Never write phrases such as "tree's shape" or "house's windows," our English teachers warned, because a tree or a house can't actually possess anything.

Were we victims of a fallacy? Or, to put it another way, were we a fallacy's victims?

Yes.

We fell for the long-standing but mistaken notion that an apostrophe attached to a noun always indicates literal ownership. This may be true in some cases ("Joan's car"), but when we speak of "Joan's neighborhood," we don't mean Joan actually owns the neighborhood; we simply mean she's connected with it in some way. Phrases such as "Joan's neighborhood," which imply connection rather than literal ownership, are called "descriptive genitives" as opposed to "possessive genitives."

And if a descriptive genitive can describe the connection of a person to something, why can't it describe the connection of an inanimate object to something, as in "tree's shape"?

Attaching *s* to inanimate objects didn't bother William Shakespeare. He used more descriptive genitives than you could shake a truncheon at: "country's fate," "heart's core," "truncheon's length."

The belief that the genitive case should be reserved for literal ownership began in the 18th century. That's when grammarians started faulting English phrases such as "king's English" because, they reasoned, the monarch in question didn't really own the language. (After they insulted these regal possessions, some of these linguists soon discovered they didn't actually own their own heads.)

Ignoring these pedants, people continued to attach apostrophes to inanimate nouns related to time and money ("ten dollars' worth," "Seven Years' War") and retained idiomatic phrases such as "stone's throw," "duty's call" and "pity's sake." And where would our "Star-Spangled Banner" be without its "dawn's early light" and "rocket's red glare"?

Generally, the ban on inanimate possessives has been a bomb bursting in air. During the past 50 years, most experts have lifted the prohibition on using apostrophes with inanimate objects, largely because it leads to wordiness. Why write "demise of the rule" when you can write "rule's demise"?

But be careful. When an inanimate possessive looks or sounds weird ("pot of coffee's freshness"), it's wise to brew up a fresh pot ("freshness of the pot of coffee").

Never use hopefully *to mean it is to be hoped*

Ah, *hopefully.* Perhaps no other word has endured so much scorn from highfalutin grammarians in recent years. With the venerable Edwin Newman leading the charge, learned linguists periodically assail the use of *hopefully* to mean one hopes or it is hoped, as in, "Hopefully, Edwin will lighten up."

Hopefully haters argue that, as an adverb, *hopefully* must modify a verb, adjective or another adverb. What word, they ask, does *hopefully* modify in this sentence: "Hopefully, Babe will hit a home run when he steps to the plate"? Does it modify *hit*? *Steps*? Why not just begin the sentence with "I hope" or "we hope" instead?

Hopefully, I can ump. The placement of *hopefully* at the beginning (or sometimes end) of the sentence tells you it modifies not a just a word or phrase but the entire sentence. *Mercifully* performs the same function in, "Mercifully, experts don't complain about other sentence-modifying adverbs."

And sometimes *hopefully* is better than "I hope" or "we hope" because the speaker is expressing not just personal hope or group hope, but a general condition of hope. Sure, we could use "it is hoped" or "one hopes" to express this ambient hope, but who wants to sound stuffy and awkward?

The fact that serious attacks on the use of *hopefully* didn't begin until the word became trendy in the 1960s suggests grammarians were objecting as much to its overuse as its misuse. Since then, revulsion toward *hopefully* has been a requirement for admission to the infernal coterie of elite grammarians whose motto is "Abandon *hopefully* all ye who enter here."

Meanwhile, the American public, in its infinite common sense, has kept right on using *hopefully* because it performs a useful function. That's why I say it's OK to use *hopefully* to mean it is hoped.

Hopefully, grammatical purists will find something else to worry about.

Never confuse shall *and* will

What's the difference between *shall* and *will?*

Luminaries no less august than God, Douglas MacArthur, the Rev. Martin Luther King Jr., and the Beatles have decreed, respectively, "Thou shalt not kill," "I shall return," "We shall overcome," and "Me shall, ma belle," respectively. And yet, if I ever announced to my bowling buddies, "I shall have a beer," they'd laugh at me till August.

What gives?

To find out, the first thing we shall do is visit grandma's attic where, near the old spinning wheel, we find some dusty old linguistic regulations.

Look! There's the antique prohibition on splitting infinitives, a rule we once vowed to never break. And there's that old-fashioned stricture, now yellow and faded, forbidding us from beginning sentences with *And*. But now we say "ick" to these rules of yore. Alas, poor yore "ick," we knew them well!

Ah, here's what we're looking for: Grandma's grammar book explaining the proper uses of *shall* and *will*. Let's blow the dust off and take a look...

Hmmmmm. Says here, three centuries ago, some English guy named John Wallis proclaimed: "With a subject in the first person, *shall* indicates future time and *will* expresses determination. With a subject in the second or third person, the opposite applies: will indicates the future and *shall* expresses determination."

Huh?

Look at it this way. According to this Wallisy policy, when Grandma says, "I will attend the Phish concert and Gramps shall go too," she means "I am determined to attend and Gramps must go too." But if she says, "I shall attend the Phish concert and Gramps will go too," she means simply, "We're going" (no obligation or determination implied). (Funny, but all my other grandmother wants to do is play Go Fish.)

Although most grandmas and grammarians have faithfully heeded these complicated *shall/will* commandments for three centuries, it's now time for these outmoded rules to sleep with the fishes.

True, we still occasionally use *shall* to imply eagle determination ("We shall prevail"), legal obligation ("The tenant shall provide a security deposit"), and regal invitation ("Shall we dance?").

But, mostly we shall simply ignore the fussy distinctions between *shall* and *will*. Shall we?

Never treat **none** *as a plural pronoun*

In fourth grade, you probably learned the word *none* is a contraction of *no one*, and thus should always take a singular verb. Because you would never say, "no one have," your well-meaning teacher told you, you shouldn't say, "none have."

Nonetheless, many of us continue to believe this *none* fiction. We're still nonplused whenever we hear *none* used with a plural verb. On occasion, this has even led to *none*-violence.

In fact, *none* has been used as a plural pronoun for at least a thousand years. Your teacher was right about one thing: the Old English *nan* (none) was indeed a contraction of *ne* (not) and *an* (one). But *nan* was never used in the singular only—not even for a nano-second.

To prove the acceptability of the plural *none*, I'll cite chapter and verse: "But none of these things move me" (Acts, 20:24). And I'll cite versatile chaps: "None of these are love letters" (W. H. Auden); "None of my sisters are coming to London" (Lewis Carroll); "None of these statements are particularly disputable" (Tom Wicker).

None of these statements are disputable, you say, but when should I treat *none* as singular and when should I treat it as plural?

Here's the easy part: If your *none* seems to mean a single item, use a singular verb; if your *none* seems to mean many items, use a plural verb.

Thus, when by *none* you mean not a single, ever-loving, cotton-picking one—not one!—you should treat *none* as a singular, as in "Of the more than 25 kids in the class, none is following the teacher's dictum." But when your *none* means more than one, treat it as a plural, as in "None of us are following the teacher's dictum."

Now you can be *none* chalant.

Never argue with your son.

The demise of these revered rules is perhaps best summarized by this dialogue between a 50-something father and a 20-something son:

Dad: In my day, splitting an infinitive or ending a sentence with a preposition would earn you a rap on the knuckles.

Lad: Well, dad, grammarians now say it's OK to occasionally split an infinitive and to end a sentence with a preposition. You'll have to knuckle under.

Dad: Well, at least all the other rules I learned survive. It's still wrong to begin a sentence with *But*.

Lad: But most grammarians now say it's not wrong. And they allow you to begin a sentence with *And*, too.

Dad: Knuckle heads! Thank goodness it's still a mistake to treat *none* as a plural.

Lad: None of the grammarians now believe *none* must always take a singular verb. They say *none* can mean not any, as well as not one, so it's OK to say, "none of them are correct."

Dad: None of them is correct! Why do they keep throwing us these knuckle balls? Soon they'll be rescinding the rule that inanimate objects can't take a possessive apostrophe.

Lad: They already have. Just check this new grammar book's chapter on possessives.

Dad: Great! The next thing you know someone will come along insisting it's fine to say "It's me" and, "That's her."

Lad: It's me. Even the strictest grammarians now concede it's artificial and stuffy to say, "It is I" and "That's she." A victim who has been assaulted with brass knuckles, for instance, wouldn't point out his assailant in a police lineup and say, "That's he!"

Dad: I feel as if *I've* been assaulted. I suppose they've tossed out the old *shall/will* rule, too. Gosh, I spent hours memorizing that one. I will never surrender to such permissiveness.

Lad: But I shall. *Will* is used in most situations now, with *shall* reserved for social or legal formalities ("Shall we dance?" "The tenant shall pay monthly rent") or strong intention ("We shall overcome.")

Dad: It is to be hoped that the rule against using *hopefully* to mean it is to be hoped still survives.

Lad: Hopefully, you're starting to get the message, Dad. Popular usage has made the use of *hopefully* as a sentence-modifying adverb acceptable.

Dad: If you tell me one more rule I learned in school is obsolete, somebody's going to get a knuckle sandwich.

Lad: How 'bout them Red Sox.

Sound Barriers

How sound is your knowledge of words that sound alike? Pull out a pen and (then, than) see if you can get (passed, past) this quiz.

1) She wrote the letter on formal (stationary, stationery).

2) The aristocrat was to the (manor, manner) born.

3) Using a camera always makes me (shudder, shutter).

4) The transplanted mountain laurel proved very (hearty, hardy).

5) Jane strained her vocal (cords, chords).

6) Congress tried to (pare, pear) down the budget.

7) Tom thought Jim's plan was (errant, arrant) nonsense.

8) The missile (honed, homed) in on its target.

Answers:

1) Stationery. When you write on stationery (paper), you want it to remain stationary (fixed in place.) Remember that *stationery* has an *e*, as in *letter*.

2) Manner. Although an aristocrat may be born on a manor (estate), the phrase "to the manner born" refers to someone's manner (way) of living.

3) Shudder. OK, OK, I deliberately threw off your focus by mentioning a camera. An icky bug makes you shudder (shake), but a shutterbug's camera has a shutter (device that opens and shuts).

4) Hardy. Anything hearty is done with the heart, with warmth, vigor and sincerity ("a hearty welcome"), while something hardy is robust,

sturdy or courageous ("a hardy explorer"). Plant this in your mind: "laurel is hardy."

5) Cords. If Jane and her friends use their vocal cords (rope-like fibers) simultaneously, they can produce chords (harmonious musical notes). Remember that the *h* in *chord* is for harmony.

6) Pare. If you pare (cut off the outer coverings) of two pears, you'll have a pair of pared pears.

7) Arrant. *Arrant* means complete or total, usually with a negative connotation, as in an "arrant fool." *Errant* means wandering or roving, as in a "knight errant."

8) Homes. A missile, like a homing pigeon, homes in on its target. When you hone a tool or your skills, you sharpen and perfect them.

Scores: 8 correct—Zounds! 6–7—You're to the manner born. 4–5—Hone your skills a bit. 0–3—Shudder.

Chapter 11—

'Pigeon' English: Coming to Terms with Animals

Whether we're composing doggerel, competing in a spelling bee or speaking pig Latin, animals bark, buzz and oink in our language. Sometimes these wee beasties are obviously zoo-"logical," as in *top dog* and *hog wild*, but sometimes they're zoo-"illogical," as in *lobster shift* and *curry favor*.

Let's explore the language zoo. Are you game?

(Humanitarian disclaimer: no actual birds, cats, dogs, frogs or fish were harmed in the writing of this chapter.)

Let slip the dogs of words

Those sultry weeks of midsummer when even the hardiest hound droops listlessly off to a shady spot on the front porch are called the *dog days*. But, despite our sympathy for these parched, poached, porched pooches, the origin of the term *dog days* has nothing to do with cooked canines.

During ancient Roman times, Sirius, the "Dog Star," rose with the sun during July and August. Taking this event seriously, the Romans referred to midsummer as "the dog days."

In modern times, even though Sirius now rises with the sun in late August, not early July, and our dog stars are named Lassie and Beethoven, we still use this term for that period when it's doggone hot.

In fact, when it comes to language, dogs have been man's and woman's best friends, contributing a *dog's breakfast* (mixed bag) of words and

153

phrases to English. Their tenacity, for instance, gives us *dogged*, their ferocity gives us *dog-eat-dog*, and their slouch gives us *hangdog*.

The terms *top dog* and *underdog* for champions and challengers, respectively, come from the days when logs were sawed over a pit by two workers. The sawyer in the pit (who got covered with sawdust) was the *underdog*, and the man who guided the saw from above was the *top dog*.

A *dog in the manger*, meaning a person who selfishly keeps others from using something he can't use himself, comes from Aesop's fable about a snarling cur who prevented oxen and horses from eating hay he couldn't eat himself.

We prescribe *hair from the dog that bit you* (an alcoholic drink) as a cure for hangovers, because it was once believed that a dog bite could be healed if hair from the canine culprit was placed on the wound. To *put on* the *dog* means to show off wealth or culture, but the exact origin of this term gives even the best etymologists paws, er…pause.

Often dogs are linked with degradation. *Doggerel* (crudely fashioned verse) is named for them, and the mild oath *doggone* is a contraction of *dog on it*. Likewise, *to go to the dogs* is to deteriorate and a *dog's life* is a miserable existence.

Given all these lowly associations, the dog days may not be so hot after all.

Straight from the horse's mouth

According to a recent "gallop" poll, few people realize the "mane" role horses have played in the origin of terms such as *marshal, get someone's goat* and *shoo-in*. Let's get the story straight from the horse's mouth. Here's Old Dobbin himself:

Howdy folks. I've toted marshals all over the Wild West looking for bad guys. But do you think anyone knows the word *marshal* comes from the Germanic words *marhaz* (horse) and *skalkaz* (servant)? Neigh!

(And, by the way, that old gray *marhaz* ain't what she used to be; now she's *mare* in English.)

The French used the word *marahskalk* to describe a royal official who rode around on a horse to enforce the king's laws (see "Rein of Terror"). Eventually, *marahskalk* became *marshal* in English

What really gets my goat is that no one realizes we horses were the first to in-"stall" the phrase *get my goat*. Goats were sometimes placed in the stables of race horses to calm and, well...stabilize them. Gamblers and their henchmen, intent on sabotaging a certain horse's chances, would sometimes try to upset the steed by stealing its goat before a big race. So to get *someone's goat* means to rile a rival.

Horse racing also gives us the expressions *shoo-in* and *win hands down*. Sometimes, when I'm running far ahead of the rest of the field, all my jockey has to do is whisper *shoo* into my ear to urge me home, making me a *shoo-in* for first place. And, if my jockey doesn't even have to raise the reins to speed me up, I win *hands down*.

When you *curry favor*, for instance, you're actually grooming Fauvel, a horse who represented duplicity in a 14th-century satirical romance. Over the centuries *Fauvel* destabilized into *favel* and then *favor*, and soon people emitting horse laughs at the CEOs bad jokes were said to be *currying favor*.

Let's do some leg work on my friend *charley horse*. There are two possible origins of this term for an upper leg cramp, both equally lame. Some say it goes back to the reign of Charles II in England, when the partially disabled veterans given jobs as night watchmen were called *charleys* because that was the king's name. By somewhat extensive extension, lame horses became known as *charleys* and muscle cramps as *charley horses*.

Others say it's the legacy of Charley, a horse who pulled a roller for the Chicago White Sox grounds crew during the 1890s. Because Charley walked with a distinctive limp, he soon became a ballpark figure, so to speak, and baseball fans soon started calling any player suffering from muscular stiffness a *charley horse*.

But in 1889, shortly before Charley rolled, a Cincinnati newspaper described a ball player's injury as a *charley horse*, so it doesn't take a lot of horse sense to realize that somebody is pulling our leg.

Now, I don't mean to be a nag, but here are two more words with horse sense. A *henchman* (*hengsman* in Middle English) was a page who held a noble's horses, while *hackney* (meaning banal, trite) comes from *hack* (a worn-out horse for hire).

"Hold your horses!" you say. "*Hack* and *hackney* refer to the coach for hire, not the horse."

But I reply: "That's putting the cart before the horse." *Hackney* originally referred to the horse itself (from Hackney, a borough of London where horses were raised).

Did someone say *burro*?

Animal crackers

- **toady**—You might assume sycophants are called *toadies* because they sit around like toads, worshipping and flattering powerful people. But the true origin of *toady* is harder to swallow.

  During the Middle Ages, people believed toads were poisonous. (Where they got that ridiculous idea, heaven knows; now we know they only cause warts.) Anyway, medieval quacks and charlatans, claiming magical powers to purge poisons, would feed a toxic toad to an assistant and then "miraculously" cure the poor fellow. These human guinea pigs were called *toad eaters* and soon the shortened form *toady* was applied to anyone who did anything a powerful person asked.

- **tarantella**—The frenzied Italian dance called the *tarantella* is named after the tarantula spider. According to Italian folklore, the only way to cure a tarantula bite was to engage in a vigorous dance, and soon this dance (often performed to the music of the rock star

Sting) became known as a *tarantella*. The word *tarantula* itself comes from the Italian city of Taranto where these poisonous critters were found. (For more information, you can visit the internet's Spider Web Site.)

- **swan song**—This term, which refers to someone's final appearance, action or work, is derived from the ancient belief that swans remained mute until their dying moment when suddenly they would sing one beautiful, sad melody before expiring; (see "Swan Lake"). Others say they sang livelier ditties; (see "Way Down upon the Swan-ee River"). Others say they just croaked.

- **beat around the bush**—In 15th-century England, it was common practice to catch songbirds for eating (see "Robin Hood"). Hunters would often sneak up on the birds at night when the flock was sleeping in a bush (see "bush league").

  (Renaissance math problem: If you hunted around the clock for one full day, and caught an average of one blackbird per hour, how many blackbirds could you bake in a pie, if pie is valued at 3.14159?)

  I'll stop beating around the bush. Hunters would spread a net over the bird-bearing bush and then beat around the bush with sticks to startle the poor creatures and make them fly into the net. By the 17th century, *beat around the bush* was being used metaphorically to mean waste time in preliminaries and avoid the central point.

- **raining cats and dogs**—This pet phrase has enjoyed a long reign and experts have whipped up a cat o' nine tales to explain its origin. It first appeared in a 1652 play by Richard "Acu-Weather" Brome ("and it shall rain…dogs and polecats") and was used again in 1783 by Jonathan "Doppler" Swift ("he was sure it would rain cats and dogs.")

  Some authorities doggedly contend the phrase was inspired by the fact that frogs and fish, snatched upward by tornadoes, sometimes fall back to earth during severe thunderstorms. (By this time, the frogs have already croaked in more ways than one.) So a storm powerful enough to lift and relocate animals as large as cats and dogs would surely be a bona "fido" catastrophe.

Some say the term's catalyst is Norse weather lore, which associates cats with storms and dogs with wind. Still others attribute this umbrella clause to claws: the resemblance of thunderstorms to fights between dogs and cats.

The most ghoulish, yet most plausible explanation literally descends to the gutter. In olden days, garbage of all kinds, including the corpses of cats and dogs, accumulated in the gutter. So when a downpour struck that was strong enough to dislodge these dead critters and float them down the street, it was said to be *raining cats and dogs.*

Pig 'meant' ation

Let's go hog wild over words and phrases of porcine origin!

- **buy a pig in a poke**—In merry olde England, a suckling pig was often brought to market in a poke (a small sack). Sometimes swindlers (in this case, "swine-dlers") would place an undersized piglet or even a cat in a poke and try to sell it sight unseen. A victim of such "hocus-poke us" was said to have bought *a pig in a poke,* and this phrase soon referred to purchasing any item without first giving it a cat scan.

- **pig iron**—Molten iron is poured from a blast furnace into a series of troughs lined up next to one another. Because the line of oblong troughs waiting to receive this liquid iron reminded workers of nursing piglets, the resulting ingots came to be called *pig iron.* Under this "litter-al" but "ironic" interpretation, the channel that conducted iron to the molds became a *sow,* and the sand in which the ingots lay was called a *pig bed.*

- **root hog or die**—When fodder for pigs was scarce, 19th-century American farmers would shout to a ravenous porker, "What ya' lookin' at me, fer? Root, hog, or die!" Whether the word *hog* is an appositive ("root, you hog, or die"), or a verb ("you can either root, or hog, or die") has been the subject of innumerable scholarly treatises. One thing is clear: the phrase means to fend for oneself or die, or, as scholars extremely desperate for research topics put it, "publish or perish."

- **as independent as a hog on ice**—The intrepid etymologist Charles Earle Funk spent many decades trying to root out the derivation of this term. He envisioned runaway pigs as they glided freely on ice; he envisioned sides of pork preserved on ice; he envisioned a new line of work.

  After following a research trail with more curlicues than a pig's tail, Funk eventually took his cue from curling, a Scottish sport in which young "loch"-invars slide heavy stones across the ice. Because an underpropelled stone that stopped halfway along the course and became frozen in the ice resembled an inert pig, this obstacle became known as a *hog*.

  Curling their lips, the Scots began describing any stubborn, self-sufficient person as being *as independent as a hog on ice*.

Buffing up buffalo

And now a dialogue between Biff and his dad, the word buff...

Biff: Dad, why do we call a person who's enthusiastic and knowledgeable about a certain subject a *buff*?

Buff: To answer your question, son, let's shuffle off to *buffalo*. *Buffalo* comes from the Greek *boubalos*, a word Europeans used for mammals such as antelopes and water buffaloes. When European explorers of North America first spotted big, shaggy bison that vaguely resembled the water buffaloes of southern Asia, they called them *buffaloes*, showing the same linguistic sloppiness they did in calling Native Americans *Indians*. So, from the point of view of semantic accuracy, there *were* some discouraging words heard on the range after all.

Biff: Don't try to buffalo me, Dad.

Buff: That's another fascinating term! Presumably, *to buffalo* someone refers to the stampeding herds of buffalo that intimidated and baffled people on the prairies. But how this plains English entered plain English we just don't know.

Anyway, hide-bound buffalo hunters bagged so many buffalo skins that people started referring to any animal skin, and even to an animal skin's yellow-brown color, as *buffalo*—or *buff* for short. Because these buffs were often used as polishing cloths, *buff* also became a verb meaning to rub or burnish.

In fact, that's the origin of the California surfer term *buff*. People who have polished their bodies through exercise or diet to achieve physical perfection are said to be *buffed* or *buff*. (Like buffalo skins, they're well tanned, too.)

And, as long as we're baring all, *buff* also came to mean human skin. That's why, when you take off your clothes, you strip *to the buff*, or in your case, to the Biff.

Biff: But I still want to know why enthusiasts are called *buffs*!

Buff: OK. In the late 19th-century, New York City's volunteer firemen were called *buffs* because they wore buff-colored coats. Soon any thrill-seeker who dashed out to watch a blaze was called a *fire buff*. Spreading like wildfire, *buff* came to mean an enthusiast on *any* subject, from the Civil War to railroads to surfing.

Biff: That's buff! I gotta go, Dad; surf's up! But thanks for the 411 on *buffalo*.

Word Buff: Bye, son.

Bulls and bears

As the bears and bulls clash on Wall Street, some hapless mutual fund managers are now asking an important question: "Do you want fries with that?"

But we, the highly-sophisticated, stock-buying public are asking an even more profound question: "Where do the stock market terms *bear* and *bull* come from?"

The answer involves a bearskin, a bubble and a Pope.

First, picture a typical bearskin trader in England during the 1600s. We'll call him Joe.

Joe has a shrewd plan:

1) Agree to sell Lord Blunderspout a bearskin for the current price of £2.

2) Delay delivery until the price of a bearskin plummets to £1.

4) Buy a bearskin for £1 and deliver it to Lord Blunderspout.

5) Pocket a profit of £1.

This risky practice of Joe and his fellow bearskin traders was soon being imitated by brokers on London's stock exchange. Traders would sell stock they didn't actually own and promise to deliver it on a certain date in the future. Then they'd pray the stock's price would drop before the delivery date so they could buy it for less than they'd been paid for it and pocket the difference.

Stock speculators using this bearskin scheme were called *bearskin jobbers* or simply *bears* (as well as a lot of other names we can't print here). Eventually, *bear* came to refer to anyone who sells stock on the expectation of a decline in its price.

But no one really knows why a bear's opposite—a trader who buys stock in hopes its price will rise—is called a *bull*. Some say it's because bears and bulls were sometimes pitted in staged fights. Some say it's because bulls hope to toss stock prices upward with their horns. Some say, "Who cares?"

We do know that the two terms appeared in print together as early as 1720. That's when the poet Alexander Pope wrote about the disastrous investment scandal known as the "South Sea Bubble":

"Come fill the South Sea goblet full;
The gods shall of our stock take care;
Europa pleased accepts the bull,
And Jove with joy puts off the bear."

In other words, if the market drops, grin and bear it. And that, by Jove, is no bull.

The worm 'terms'

To bee or not to bee.

That is the question facing students trying to decide whether or not to participate in spelling bees.

These savvy savants must determine whether 'tis nobler in the mind to suffer the slings and arrows of spelling *outrageous*, or to take arms against a *c* of troubles in *cacciatore*.

But why is a social gathering where people combine work, competition and amusement, such as husking, quilting or spelling, called a *bee*? If you've always thought, as I had, that such events were named for the busy, sociable insect known as a *bee*, you've bumbled.

In fact, the human type of *bee* probably traces its "bee"line to the old British dialectical term *bean*, which meant voluntary help given to a farmer by his neighbors. Linguistic *bean* stalkers believe *bean* comes from the Middle English *bene*, meaning extra service by a tenant to his lord, and, before that, from the Old English *ben* (prayer), which may explain why participants in a spelling bee pray so much.

Another linguistic "term might" (a term that might be infested with bugs, but isn't) is *wormwood*. In fact, there's not even any *wood* in the name of this shrub, whose bitter leaves produce the alcoholic drink absinthe.

Wormwood is related to the German *wermut,* a combination, not of *worm* and *wood,* but of *wer* (man) and *mut* (courage). It's so named because the absinthe from its leaves was thought to be (or not to be) an aphrodisiac that gave a man amative courage.

Put simply, absinthe did not foster abstinence. (And try saying that sentence after a few glasses of absinthe.)

Wormwood brings us back to Hamlet. In the play within a play devised by Hamlet to catch the conscience of a king, the player queen proclaims that widows betray their first husbands by remarrying.

Aye, there's the rub. For this is exactly what Hamlet's mother has done by marrying the brother of her dead husband. Recognizing the bitter truth of the player queen's assertion, Hamlet whispers, "Wormwood, wormwood."

Gorilla warfare

For some zooey reason, words related to animals are particularly susceptible to beastly misuse. Let's stop this monkey business before we're all speaking "pigeon" (pidgin) English.

- **gorilla warfare**—This phrase is the 800-lb. gorilla of animal word mistakes. What's meant, of course, is *guerrilla.* A diminutive of *guerra* (Spanish for war), *guerrilla* denotes a member of an irregular military unit that operates in small bands and uses surprise raids to harass an enemy.

  Gorilla, meaning a large, anthropoid ape, has nothing to do with *guerrilla.* It apes *gorillai,* the name given by the Carthaginian navigator Hanno to the hairy, humanoid creatures he spotted during a voyage along the west coast of Africa in the fifth or sixth century B.C.

  Because both words are pronounced exactly the same (gah-RILL-ah), and guerrilla warfare is a brutish affair that often occurs in a jungle, it's easy to see why there are so many military *gorillas* in our midst.

- **Welsh rarebit**—This Americanized version of the English *Welsh rabbit* (a dish of melted cheese, and milk, cream or ale, served on toast or crackers), prompts some language purists to pull out their hare. Grammatical big cheese H. W. Fowler, for example, roundly thumps *welsh rarebit* as a pretentious term used by restaurants to impart elegance to an everyday snack. But his opponents rabbit punch *welsh rabbit*, contending that it falsely suggests the presence of bunny meat.

  While this rabid controversy strikes me as splitting hares, I'll place my rabbit's foot firmly in my mouth and hippity hop to *Welsh rabbit*.

- **Doberman Pincher**—Anyone whose leg has been pinched by the jaws of a Doberman Pinscher (PIN-shar) might be excused for calling this intimidating breed a *Doberman Pincher* (PINCH-er). It's named for the 19th-century German dog breeder Ludwig Dobermann who crossbred Pinschers, a type of German terrier, with other species to create his new breed of grrrrrr-illa.

Cat Scan

Meee-oowww!
Pick the correct verbs on this quiz and you'll avoid a grammatical "cat"astrophe:

1) The cat (use, used) to roam at night.
2) Did the cat (use, used) to roam at night?
3) The cat is carrying what (look, looks) like two mice in its mouth.
4) What (distinguishes, distinguish) the cat (is, are) its white paws.
5) He is one of the cats that (likes, like) to be touched while eating.
6) He is the only one of the cats that (likes, like) to be touched while eating.

7) Either the calico cat or the striped cats (loves, love) fish.

8) One or more of the cats (loves, love) catnip.

Answers:

1) Used. Even though the phrase "use to," when spoken, sounds almost the same as "used to," the past tense verb *used* is correct.

2) Use. "Did use" means the same thing as *used*, just as "did meow" means the same as *meowed*. You wouldn't write, "did meowed," so don't write, "did used."

3) Look. Just reverse the sentence: The mice are carrying what looks like a cat in their mouths. Oops, wrong kind of reverse! Two mice look like what the cat is carrying in its mouth.

4) Either "What distinguishes the cat is its white paws," or, "What distinguish the cat are its white paws." Some experts may caterwaul over either construction, but whatever you do, don't go calico. Both verbs must be plural or both must be singular.

5) Like. Sentences using "one of the," or "one of those" can create grammatical cataclysms. When in doubt, just reverse the sentence this way: "Of the cats that like to be touched while eating, he is one."

6) Likes. Using *only* stresses the cat's singularity, so use the singular verb form.

7) Love. If one part of a compound subject separated by *or* is singular and one part is plural, the verb agrees with the nearer subject ("striped cats love").

8) Love. Again, in compound subjects separated by *or*, the verb agrees with the nearer subject ("more love catnip").

Chapter 12—

Gaffes for Laughs: Howlers, Boners and Bloopers

When it comes to grammar and usage, we all make misteaks, er…mistakes. Some call them "howlers"; others call them "boners"; I call them "bloopers."

Readers and friends collect these gems from newspapers, magazines and other publications and send them to me, and many of their finds are included in this chapter.

But before we turn to contemporary gaffes, let's revisit the original matriarch of mistakes—Mrs. Malaprop, the meddlesome aunt in Richard Sheridan's 1775 comedy *The Rivals* who continually confuses one word with another.

With Malaprop toward none

It's from Mrs. Malaprop, in fact, that we get the word *malapropism*, meaning the ludicrous misuse of words. Sheridan derived Mrs. Malaprop's name from the French phrase *mal à propos*, literally meaning badly to the purpose or, as Mrs. Malaprop herself might put it, "badly to the porpoise." Actually, we should pity Mrs. Malaprop. No, not because she commits "erroneous" assault on the language by making usage "giraffes" and substituting similar-sounding words for the intended ones. Not because she "intervents" new words ("pernicity") and reverses time "sequins" ("anticipate the past"). And not even because she's "inflatulated" with long, Latinate words she thinks will impress others.

No, we should pity Mrs. Malaprop because no one has ever repre-hended, er…apprehended how much wisdom is hidden in her "mistakes." In this "urology," I come to "braise" Mrs. Malaprop, not to "parry" her.

When Mrs. Malaprop, for instance, says, "my affluence (influence) over my niece is very small," she's right on the money. Her niece commands a more "voluptuous" fortune than she does. And when she urges her niece to "illiterate" (obliterate) the low-ranking Ensign Beverly from her stream of "conscientiousness," we can read between the lines that she thinks Beverly can't read the lines themselves.

Similarly, by referring to "the contagious (contiguous) countries," Mrs. Malaprop is subtly "intimidating" her aversion to disease-ridden foreign nations, just as her demand for "no delusions (allusions) to the past" suggests her justifiable "septicism" about the "voracity" of the narratives she's hearing. When she says someone "can tell you all the perpendiculars (particulars)" of some murders, she's simply "eluding" to the fact that the bodies of the victims now lie at right angles to the upright positions they occupied when alive.

And, please, let no more disapprobation of her "inflamous" metaphor "he is the very pineapple of politeness" be doled out. Here, she is merely "refruiting" someone else's "illusion" to an orange tree. Similarly, scholars and other stuffy "pedicures" say her simile "she's as headstrong as an alle-gory (alligator) on the banks of the Nile" is a crock. Don't they know she's referring to the Egyptian sphinx, a statuesque allegory with a very strong head indeed?

But what about her many "oblivious errors," such as her claim, "I have proof suppository (positive) of it"? Even here, her linguistic rectitude needs no corrective. She's merely "inserting" her authority

So, instead of casting "aspirations" on Mrs. Malaprop, we should shower her with "condiments." She is, in fact, a commanding "distress" of language who, to use her own words, gives us "joy infinitesimal."

Harried Headlines

"British Left Waffles on Falklands"
"Father of 9 Fined $100 for Failing To Stop"
"Fish Lurk in Streams"
Ah, the headline!—that blazing bolt of journalistic lightning, crackling with precision, intensity and clarity!

Headlines, of course, epitomize the highest and most cherished standards of journalism: integrity, accuracy, fairness and the ability to cram 12 words into a six-inch-wide space.

Which may explain why so many headlines give us laugh lines.

Sometimes, as in "British Left Waffles on Falklands," there's ambiguity about a word's part of speech:

Chinese Protest Mushrooms

Helicopter Powered by Human Flies

·Press Tours Ravaged City

Why You Want Sex Changes with Age

U.S. Ships Head to Somalia

Doctors Help Torch Victim

Voter Fears Alert Politicians

Lawyers To Offer Poor Free Advice

Fine Young Man Convicted of Misdemeanor

U.S. Advice: Keep Drinking Water from Sewers

Vicious Animal Calls Up

Oldest Survivors of Titanic Sinking

Jersey City Cop Trips under Scrutiny

Clinton Visits Hurt Soldiers

In other headlines, the double meaning of a word or phrase causes us to double over:

Cuban Military Jets Attacked with Relish, Transcript Says

Chef Throws His Heart into Helping Feed Needy

Here's How You Can Lick Doberman's Leg Sores

Lawmakers Back Train through Iowa

Kids Make Nutritious Snacks

Police Can't Stop Gambling

Lansing Residents Can Drop off Trees

Grandmother of Eight Makes Hole in One

Calf Born to Farmer with Two Heads

And some heads simply leave us shaking our heads:

Mayor Says DC Is Safe Except for Murders

Dog That Bit 2 People Ordered To Leave Town

Man Says Body Is His Wife but She Tells Police It Isn't

Three Ambulances Take Blast Victim to Hospital

High-Crime Areas Said To Be Safer

Nudist Group Donates Clothing for Victims

But my favorite headlines are those that state the obvious. In this "Stop the Presses!" category we find:

Experts Are Sure the Dow Will Either Rise or Decline

Don't Leave Kids Alone with Molester

Some Teens Have Air of Defiance

Blow to Head Is Common Cause of Brain Injury

Job Growth Reduces Unemployment

Alcohol Ads Promote Drinking

Malls Try To Attract Shoppers

Missouri Gas Chamber Is Unsafe

Official: Only Rain Will Cure Drought

Larger Kangaroos Leap Farther, Researchers Find

Mixed Metaphors

In our scramble to mold metaphors that don't go down the tubes like lead balloons, we often end up with unsavory omelets. But, hey, if you want to make *Hamlet*, you have to break eggs. Yes, even Shakespeare, that wily master of metaphors, sometimes mixed them.

In Hamlet's famous soliloquy, for instance, the princely protagonist wonders aloud (in a metaphor that shouldn't be allowed) whether to "take arms against a sea of troubles," leaving the confused playgoer wondering how well the great Dane's sword and shield would stand up to the North Sea in a 15-round "tidal" bout.

Now let's peer at some other metaphors that give us the shakes:

"The nomination looked like a feather in our caps, and now we have to wipe the egg off our face." Did the same prolific bird produce both the feather and egg? (Perhaps, in true Yankee tradition, he stuck a feather in his cap and called it egg noodle.)

"The first shoe came from Sen. Dianne Feinstein…The second shoe came from the White House…The *third* shoe fell at roughly the same time." Perhaps the cobbler of this metaphor never lived in an apartment beneath another tenant, or perhaps he had some very strange upstairs neighbors (maybe even a four-footed "NAAAAY…bor" like Mr. Ed). Somehow the concept of waiting for the other shoe to drop got lost in the shuffle.

"We are still ascending the learning curve, but the goal posts are being continually moved." Maybe the quarterback threw a curve ball.

Vicious Verbs

Many of the most egregious mistakes go from bad to verb:

"Grown men shuttered at the reality of such a momentous event." Unless those grown men were photographers, that sentence is a groaner. (*shuddered*)

"Mike Marley…led chants of 'Here! Here!'" Great Marley's Ghost! It's "Hear, Hear!"

"He heard his 12-year-old Irish setter, Whitney, wretching as a result of the gas." And after *retching*, Whitney surely felt wretched.

"Regular readers of the New York Times will need to steal themselves for the hurricane of hyperbole ." Will all those readers really kidnap themselves? (*steel*)

"It didn't phase him." Though he did go through a *fazed* phase.

"Airline pilots tend to euphemize plane crashes with terms like 'auguring in.'" Mistaking *auger* (to bore into wood) for *augur* (to bore into *would*) augurs poorly for the fate of both carpentry and correct usage.

"Neither of the Clintons were charged with wrongdoing." And neither *was* charged with subject-verb disagreement.

"Bomb found by children in library diffused." Changing two letters would have *defused* this usage bomb.

"Didn't she used to write a newspaper column?" The past tense *didn't* makes the past tense *used* redundant. Try, "Didn't she *use* to write a newspaper column?"

"Disney's *Hunchback* abandons Hugo's tragic ending, in which the Gypsy Esmeralda is hung." This sentence, unlike Esmeralda, was not well executed; someone who's executed by hanging is *hanged*.

This caption appeared under a photo of Jack Kemp with his arms raised in triumph: "Jack Kemp exalts Sunday after completing a pass to a former teammate." Jack Kemp may be an exalted ex-quarterback, but here he was *exulting* (rejoicing), not *exalting* (to elevate or glorify someone).

"Giant 'love-in' gatherings—featuring music, light shows and the flaunting of drug laws." If you've got it, *flaunt* it, but if you hate it (as the love-in participants undoubtedly did drug legislation), *flout* it (defy it).

"That could help staunch the market's bleeding, analysts said." Even staunch linguistic conservatives can't seem to *stanch* the use of *staunch* for *stanch*.

"British battle with EU could sew chaos." We're in stitches. (*sow*)

"Neither [candidate] mustard enough votes to capture the one-year seat." Though one contender reportedly tried desperately to ketchup with the other. (*mustered*)

"Lincoln poured over the map of Virginia." Unless Abe spilled something on the maps, he *pored* over them.

"[When we're together] we all digress to about age ten." Yup. We get off the subject and start telling stories about fourth grade. Try *regress*.

"Charges have been allegated against Hillary [Clinton]." The swamp of Whitewater is apparently teeming with *allegators*.

"The Connecticut River has overflown [and] will not rescind for several days." Unless that river is a jet stream, its pilot's license should be rescinded. (*overflowed, receded*)

From a car ad: "Ford spent 2.8 billion dollars to try and make an Accord." The experts are in accord: "try and make" implies that trying and making are two different actions. Try to use "try to."

"There's powerboats...there's free clinics on fishing and diving." And there *are* mistakes.

Noxious Nouns

Many errors involving nouns should be denounced:

"There appears to be a glutton of outfielders on the market." And can that guy eat! (*glut*)

"The dye is cast." A blooper to die for. (*die*)

"Having a cathode tube inserted into his groin so dye could be injected." Ouch! He'd prefer a catheter, but I guess the "dye" is cast.

"The car had a new type of rotisserie engine." Great, if you want to play chicken. (*rotary*)

"There is a split within the organization, though, regarding what the *tact* will be." One misguided faction favors *tact*; their opponents say *tack*.

Describing a baseball pitcher's view of a batter: "the poor sole 60 feet, six inches away." There's something fishy about that. (*soul*)

"...the single mature cell removed from the utter of an adult sheep." Baaaah! (*udder*)

"Highly touted quarterback Donovan McNabb and SU's passing game were out of sink." Apparently their whole game went down the drain. (*sync*)

"I have a bent sense of humor with a pension for bad puns." And no doubt some of those bad puns should be retired. (*penchant*)

"Samper claims he was unaware of the drug cash." And apparently unaware that a stash of drugs, while worth a lot of cash, is still a *cache*.

"We're very concerned about these type of allegations." And we're concerned about these *types* of errors as well.

"Ms. Farrow discovered [photographs] on a mantle at Mr. Allen's apartment." A structure over a fireplace, whether Woody or not, is a *mantel*.

"Less than half of the residents have a high school degree." A two-fer! "*Fewer* than half of the residents have high school *degrees*."

"My son-in-law will be joining me in business. In lieu of this, we are offering this special." In *view* of this, my son-in-law will be my chief lieutenant.

"The genre has now taken a thriller turn, with lawyers in daring-do situations." Lawyers in thrillers may do daring things, but it's *derring-do*.

"Brown was assigned to a prison camp where he soon earned trustee status and was allowed to work without shackles." We're shackled with the fact that a trusted convict who earns special privileges is a *trusty*.

"No woman should have to risk her piece of mind." Let me give you a piece of my mind: Try *peace* of mind.

"We personally prepare all meals from fresh ingredients, so we ask you for your patients." Were they preparing a cannibalistic feast for a doctors' convention? (*patience*)

"[This movie] is a shoe-in to get overlooked for an Oscar!" It must have been a sole-searching film. (*shoo-in*)

"I have never been in such constant term oil." I've heard of hot water, but...(*turmoil*)

From an obituary: "She is survived by one daughter and three sins." Apparently, all deadly. (*sons*)

"Mom's love roses!" And, after her kids stopped inserting unnecessary apostrophes into plural nouns, Mom's love rose. (*Moms*)

"That's the amount of households that would have noticed your ad." To say nothing of the number of readers who might have noticed this improper use of *amount*. Use *number* for plural countable items ("number of readers") and *amount* for singular mass nouns ("amount of money").

"The substance was crushed with a mortar and pedestal." Not to put accuracy on a pedestal, but this mis-rendering of "*mortar and pestle*" is crushing.

"The prisoner was released on his own reconnaissance." But, after the judge conducted a reconnaissance of the dictionary, he was released on his own *recognizance*.

"Such are the vagrancies of New England weather." Apparently we've had some bum weather lately. (*vagaries*)

From an article about refrigerator magnets: "I found about 20 of them on my truck, under the hood, in the door jam." Sounds like a refrigerator magnet jamb-oree. (*jamb*)

From an ad for a device to keep sparrows out of bluebird houses: "Don't let your hard work and patience go to waist." Give that over"bird"ened sentence a tummy tuck. (*waste*)

Addled Adjectives

Adjectives can also induce abject despair:

"I'm sure those of you who read last week's Files have been waiting with baited breath." Yes, but those earthworms left a bad taste in our mouths. (*bated*)

"A well-healed organization." The well-heeled shoes its well-*heeled* members wear must be orthopedic.

"If he doesn't respond well enough to the drugs, a more evasive procedure would be the next option." Maybe those drugs contained truth serum. (*invasive*)

"Suspects move quickly from place to place, sometimes using several stationery phones, pagers and mobile phones." Those new stationery phones are really pushing the envelope! Try *stationary*.

From instructions on how to install the exhaust system of a clothes dryer: "See pages 3 & 4 for exhausting details." I'm just too tired to read them now.

From a real estate ad: "Duel closets and track lighting are an added bonus." Closets, no doubt, where only epées and pistols are kept. (*dual*)

"The building's sorted story may have a happy ending." And this *sordid* usage has to stop.

"[He] handled one of the company's plumb assignments—covering the Oakland Raiders." Was Milt Plum on the team? (*plum*)

"First Amendment absolutists are loathe to admit it." I'm loath to admit this, but I loathe tricky spelling distinctions like this. The adjective is *loath*; the verb is *loathe*. Memory trick: both *loathe* and *verb* contain an *e*.

"Join us for hot muled cider." It really packs a kick. (*mulled*)

From a news story on the decline of baseball: "So many fans are not just hurt; they're disinterested. Baseball is no longer worth their time." As a disinterested (impartial) umpire would say, "Yaaaaahr out!" Many fans are *uninterested* (not interested).

From a letter by an official of a security-alarm company: "I must apologize for the erogenous invoice sent to you for the November 3rd service call." Did the company bill and coo? (*erroneous*)

From a scene in a best-selling novel in which a body is discovered: "They immediately recognize Gault's grizzly handiwork." Unless Gault is a bear, it should be *grisly*.

Adversarial Adverbs

We exhibit our poor power to adverb or detract:

"All these services are not available everywhere." Yes, we have no services. Try, "Not all these services are available everywhere."

"Freeman, who has turned in riveting performances in hits such as *Seven* and *Unforgiven*, is only earning $6 million a movie." If only this placement of *only* could be unforgiven. Technically, "he's only earning $6 million," means he's only earning it, as opposed to borrowing it or finding it. Try "he's earning only $6 million a movie."

Pronated Pronouns

"We do have a lot of time on hour hands." And those hands are covered with second-hand gloves. (*our*)

"That girl who's name you just can't seem to remember." And don't forget that girl *whose* grammar book you borrowed in high school.

"The Gladwin Soil Conservation District has ruled against there request." There is no *there* there. (*their*)

"Consider what your neighbor is writing, just as you would want he or she to consider what you have to say." Yes, I would want he to consider it. (*him* or *her*)

"Your approved for financing." Though we hope you're aware of the difference between *your* and *you're*.

Once upon a time

You've heard of politically correct bedtime stories? Repair the errors in each of these sentences, and you'll hear a grammatically correct bedtime story:

1) Carrying her basket of goodies, Little Red Riding Hood walked toward her grandmother's house.

2) Strolling through the woods, scary noises startled her.

3) Suddenly she was accosted by a wolf, and he asked where she was going.

4) Little Red told the wolf she was going to a house which intrigued him.

5) Rushing to the house, the wolf devoured the grandmother with a devious smile and put on her bedclothes.

6) Upon arriving, Little Red said, "Grandma, your eyes, nose and teeth have grown massively."

7) "All the better to eat you with!" the wolf roared, and, assuming this would frighten Little Red, jumped suddenly out of bed.

Answers:

1) Strict grammarians would tell you not to use a pronoun (*her*) before its antecedent ("Little Red Riding Hood"). Rewrite: "Little Red Riding Hood, carrying her basket of goodies, walked toward her grandmother's house."

2) "Strolling through the woods" is a dangling participle; it would seem to describe "noises and sounds," but "noises and sounds" can't

stroll. Rewrite: "Strolling through the woods, she was startled by scary noises."

3) This sentence is smoother when its second part is subordinated to the first. Rewrite: "Suddenly she was accosted by a wolf, who asked where she was going."

4) Was the wolf intrigued by this particular house? Rewrite: "When Little Red told the wolf she was going to a house, he was intrigued."

5) Who had the devious smile, the wolf or the grandmother? Rewrite: "The wolf rushed to the house, and with a devious smile, devoured the grandmother and put on her bedclothes."

6) Here *grown* expresses, not an action, but a state of being, so it should be followed by an adjective, not an adverb. Rewrite: "'Grandma, your eyes, nose and teeth have grown massive.'"

7) What did he think would frighten Little Red, roaring or jumping? Rewrite: "'All the better to eat you with!'" the wolf roared. Assuming a sudden leap would frighten Little Red, he jumped out of bed."

About the Author

Rob Kyff is the language columnist for the *Hartford Courant,* as well as a teacher, editor and writer. His column is nationally syndicated by Tribune Media Services and appears regularly in several newspapers, including the *Detroit Free Press, San Jose Mercury News* and *Memphis Commercial Appeal.*

A native of Armonk, New York, Mr. Kyff earned a B.A. at Amherst College and an M.A. in American studies at the University of Minnesota. He has taught English and history at Kingswood-Oxford School in West Hartford, Connecticut, since 1977 and also served as the school's director of public affairs, editor of its alumni magazine, and advisor to its student newspaper.

His essays have appeared in many newspapers, including the *Washington Post, Chicago Tribune, Boston Globe* and *Baltimore Sun,* and his articles have appeared in *Reader's Digest, American History* and *Northeast.* He also contributed to *Speaking Freely—A Guided Tour of American English from Plymouth Rock to Silicon Valley,* published by Oxford University Press in 1997.

He lives in West Hartford, Connecticut, with his wife and daughter.